M. ADAMI

Peter Bell B.Ed. (Ho

ELECTRICITY and MAGNETISM

Photocopiable Scientific Investigations for pupils

Published by:

"TOPICAL RESOURCES"

Electricity & Magnetism Photocopiable Scientific Experiments & Investigations is available from all good Educational Bookshops and by mail order from:

TOPICAL RESOURCES,
P.O. BOX 329,
BROUGHTON,
PRESTON,
LANCASHIRE
PR3 5LT

Topical Resources publishes a range of Educational Materials for use in Primary Schools and Pre-School Nurseries and Playgroups.

FOR LATEST CATALOGUE Tel/Fax 01772 863158

Printed in Great Britain for "Topical Resources", publishers of Educational Materials, P.O. Box 329, Broughton, PRESTON, PR3 5LT (Telephone 01772 863158) by T.Snape & Company Ltd., Boltons Court, Preston, Lancashire.

Typeset by Janet Nielsen, White Cross Network, White Cross, Lancaster.

First Published April 1991. Second Edition November 1995.

ISBN 1 872977 01 4

INTRODUCTION

How the Book is organised
This book contains twelve photocopiable science investigations at four different levels of ability. Each investigation is four pages long and includes background information, experiments to carry out, questions to answer and problems to solve. At the back of the book can be found detailed teacher's notes and worked examples.

Worked examples
The worked examples have been included to demonstrate to the reader the type of responses the teacher might expect. However, it must be realised that Primary Science is not an exact art and a variety of responses may be taken as being correct. What is marked as correct in individual cases is a matter for the teacher's own professional judgment. The examples given SHOULD NOT be used as answer sheets.

Organising the activities
Twelve pupil investigations of varying degrees of difficulty are included on the theme of "Electricity and Magnetism". It is envisaged that these investigations could be used to provide the Experimental Science element of a wider primary school topic on Electricity and Magnetism which may last for about half a term. It is not envisaged that every pupil will be involved in every investigation. It is more likely that small groups of 2 to 6 children will carry out 3 or 4 investigations and then report back their findings to the rest of the class. The teacher will play an important role in bringing together all of the information reported and drawing out the underlying scientific ideas.

Presentation of finished work
The old fashioned virtues of neatness and accuracy (which in the author's opinion, can so easily be lost when using worksheets) may be maintained by either (i) working a "rough" worksheet first in pencil which is corrected and then written up in ink on a second worksheet or (ii) using a "rough/ draft book" for the original work and again writing a final report on the worksheet in ink.

Levels of ability
The author has attempted to grade the investigations in line with the level descriptions found within the attainment targets. As this is still a relatively new concept in primary science, the teacher should recognise that, although every attempt has been made to make sure the gradings are accurate, small differences of opinion may occur.

Grouping of pupils
Grading the difficulty of investigations will challenge the teacher to think carefully about grouping the children. The teacher may have groups of more able children working on the higher levels and groups of less able children working on the lower levels. Alternatively, mixed ability groups may attempt all levels of activity with the teacher observing the contributions made by individual members of the group. Many variations on this theme are possible.

Reading age and Level 2 activities
The author recognises that less able or younger children working on Level 2 may need adult help with reading the text and organising their investigations.

The 12 Electricity and Magnetism Investigations are:

(1) **WHAT IS A MAGNET? - Level 2**
(2) **IS ELECTRICITY SAFE? - Level 2**
(3) **CAN ELECTRICITY STAND STILL? - Level 3**
(4) **HOW CAN YOU MAKE A SIMPLE CIRCUIT? - Level 3**
(5) **HOW DOES A SWITCH WORK? - Level 3**
(6) **WHAT IS A WIRE? - Level 3**
(7) **HOW CAN ELECTRICITY HELP US? (Part 1) - Level 4**
(8) **HOW CAN ELECTRICITY HELP US? (Part 2) - Level 4**
(9) **HOW CAN SWITCHES CONTROL ELECTRICAL DEVICES? - Level 4**
(10) **WHAT ARE LOGIC GATES? - Level 5**
(11) **CAN YOU CONSTRUCT A CIRCUIT FROM A PLAN? - Level 5**
(12) **CAN YOU VARY THE FLOW OF ELECTRICITY IN A CIRCUIT? - Level 5**

Specialist equipment needed for all 12 investigations to function simultaneously.

BATTERIES

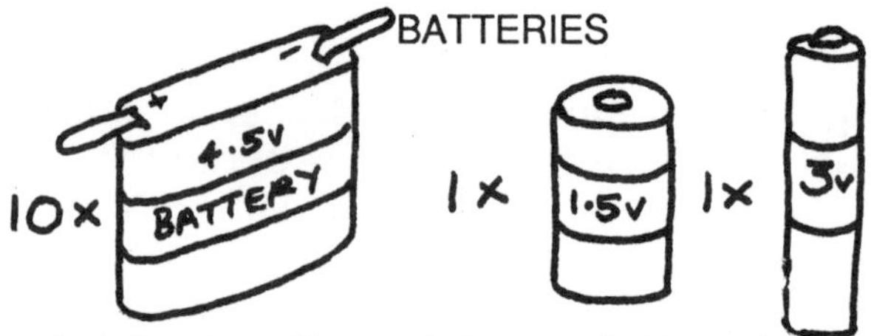

4.5volt flat-shaped battery is best used with terminals bent back - obtain locally.

ELECTRIC MAGNET

8cm nail wrapped tightly with 1m plastic coated wire held in place by sellotape.

WIRES

Thin plastic covered wire with bare ends.

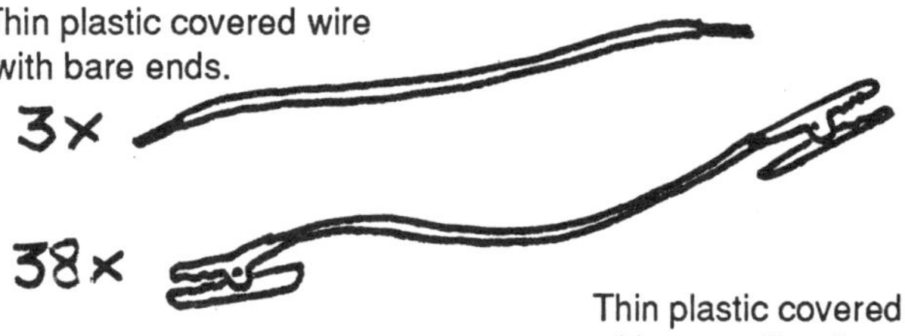

Thin plastic covered wire with crocodile clips.

BUZZER

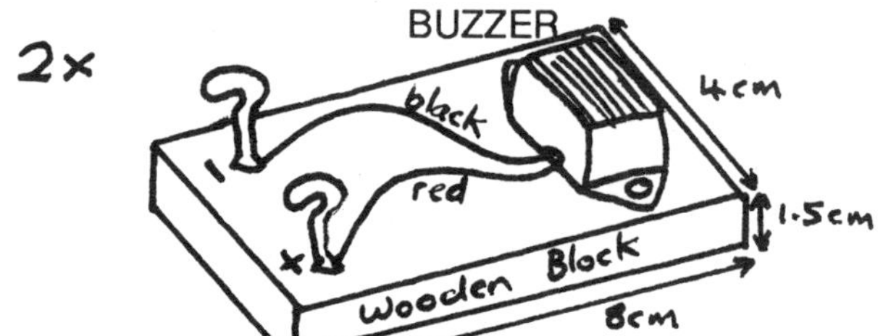

Buzzer screwed to wooden block with wires connected to brass-cup hooks marked + or -

TORCH BULBS

2.5volt bulb + spares

3.5volt bulb + spares

ELECTRIC BELL

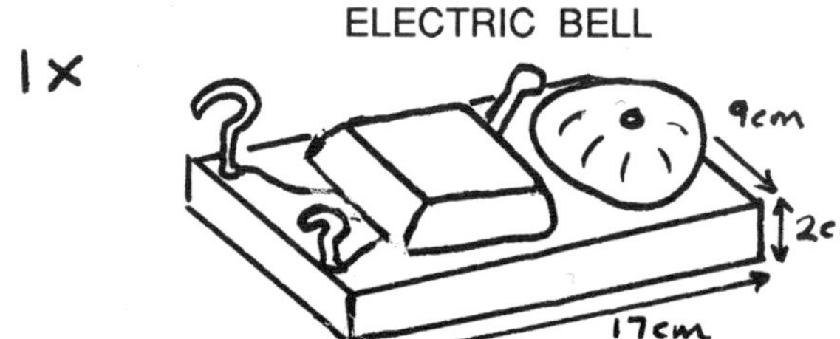

Electric door bell screwed to wooden block with wires connected to brass cup-hooks.

BULB HOLDER

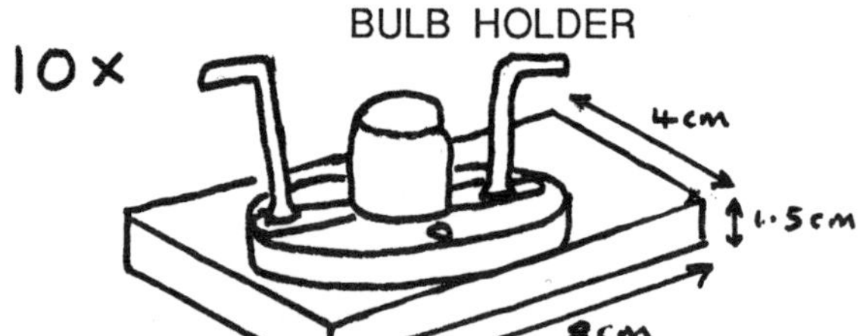

Bulb holder screwed to wooden block through connector plates using brass cup hooks.

ELECTRIC MOTOR

Small 1.5 - 4.5v electric motor fitted with push fit plastic pulley.

MAGNETS

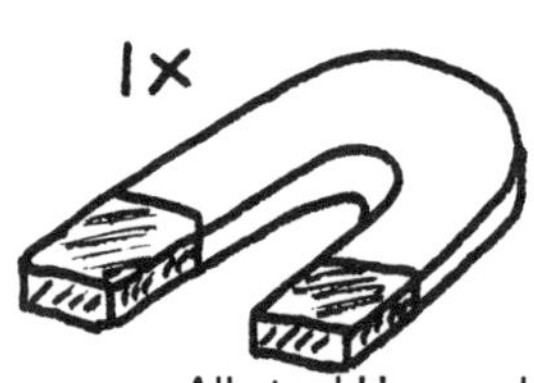

Bar magnets.

All steel Horse-shoe shaped magnet.

PUSH/CLICK SWITCH

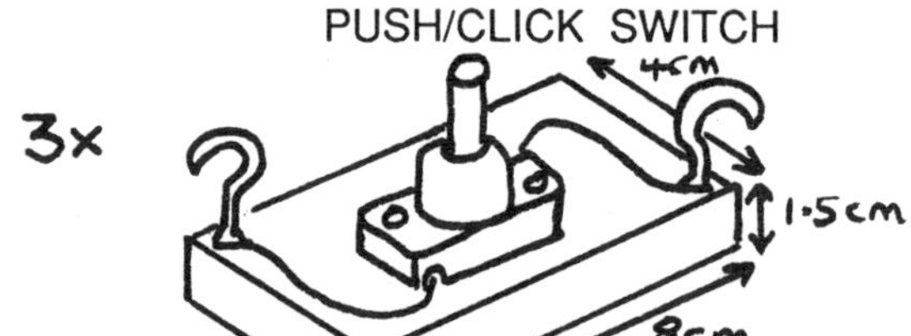

Push click switch screwed to wooden block with wires connected to brass cup-hooks.

PAPER-CLIP SWITCH

Paper-clip opened up held by brass-cup hook and drawing pin - touches another drawing pin and cup-hook when pressed.

ELECTRIC BELL GAME

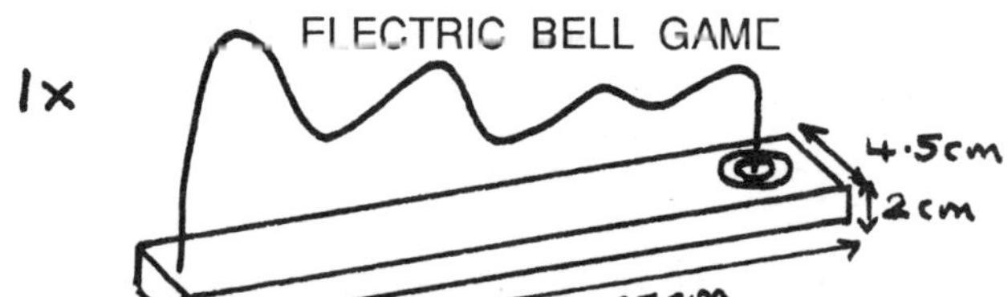

Section of metal coat hanger bent and pushed into holes in wooden block with copper washer.

WHAT IS A MAGNET?

A magnet is a piece of iron or steel that will attract other pieces of iron to itself. A magnet has an invisible pull called magnetism. This invisible force pulls some things towards the magnet. The strongest parts of a magnet are the ends. These are called poles. Magnets come in different shapes and sizes, the most common being bar magnets and horse-shoe magnets.

Experiment 1 - Which things are attracted to magnets?

Find 10 small objects. Hold a bar magnet near each one in turn. Write in the space below which are pulled by the magnet and which are not. Now start your report.

Date: ____________________

Title: ____________________

Picture of what you did

I needed ____________________

Things pulled by the magnet	Things not pulled by the magnet

I think the things pulled by the magnet were made of ____________________

If a bar magnet is held near another bar magnet ____________________

____

Experiment 2 - Which is the strongest part of a magnet?

Find a bar magnet, a horseshoe magnet and a large box of paper clips. Count how many paper clips are lifted by different parts of each magnet. Start your report.

Date: ____________________

Title: ____________________

Picture of what you did

I needed ____________________

____

One end of the bar magnet lifted ____________________

The opposite end of the bar magnet lifted ____________________

The middle of the bar magnet lifted ____________________

The ends of the horseshoe magnet lifted ____________________

The curved part of the horseshoe magnet lifted ____________________

I think the strongest parts of a magnet are ____________________ because ______

____

Questions to answer

1) What is a magnet? ____

____

2) Is a magnet sticky to touch? ____

____

3) Can you see magnetism? ____

____

4) What does the word attract mean? __________________________________

____

5) What is the name given to the strongest part of a magnet? _______________

____

6) Name some jobs a magnet could be used for. _________________________

____

____

Problems to solve

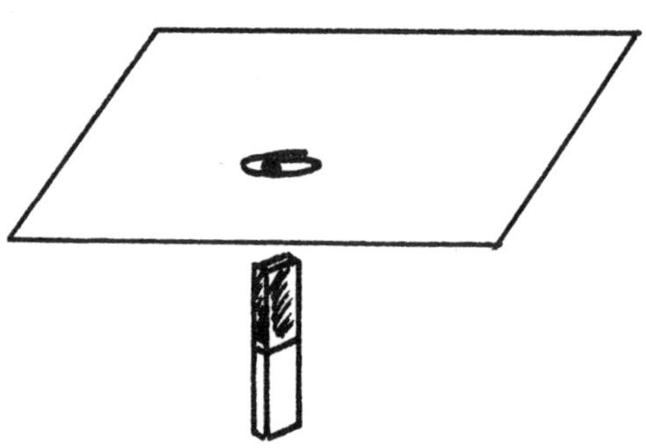

Can magnets work through materials such as paper or card?

How does a magnet effect a direction compass? Why?

Are all magnets the same strength?

IS ELECTRICITY SAFE?

Electricity is safe as long as you take care and think about what you are doing. Torch and radio batteries are perfectly safe. Car batteries can be dangerous and should not be touched. Mains electricity in the house is very dangerous and should never be played with. Overhead electrical wires are extremely dangerous. You should not even go near these.

Find Out - What is electricity used for in your home?

Write the names of 10 things which use electricity at home. Draw a small picture of each one. Write a sentence about the job each one does.

Name	Picture	Job
____________		A ____________ is used for ____________ ____________
____________		A ____________ is used for ____________ ____________
____________		A ____________ is used for ____________ ____________
____________		A ____________ is used for ____________ ____________
____________		A ____________ is used for ____________ ____________
____________		A ____________ is used for ____________ ____________
____________		A ____________ is used for ____________ ____________
____________		A ____________ is used for ____________ ____________
____________		A ____________ is used for ____________ ____________
____________		A ____________ is used for ____________ ____________

Electricity Safety Quiz

Is it safe to		Answer Yes or No
	Switch on a light with wet hands?	
	Play with a torch battery?	
	Let a baby play near an electric fire?	
	Push in a plug with wet hands?	
	Poke things into a wall socket?	
	Play with a battery powered toy car?	
	Fly a kite near overhead wires?	
	Use an iron with damaged wires?	
	Stand an electric kettle in a puddle?	
	Touch the metal parts of a plug when it is plugged into a wall socket?	
	Switch on an electric light?	
	Use a cracked or broken plug?	
	Play with a model railway or racing car set?	
	Play football near overhead wires or by an electricity sub-station?	

Use the next page to make up your own poster to warn people of the dangers of electricity.

BEWARE

ELECTRICITY CAN

CAN ELECTRICITY STAND STILL?

If you use a battery to light a small bulb, electricity moves inside the wires. This is called electric current. If you rub a balloon on a woollen sleeve the balloon will be able to attract light pieces of paper. You will have made <u>Static Electricity</u> - electricity that stays in the same spot. Static electricity can also be made by rubbing plastic on wool or combing your hair very quickly. It can even make your hair stand on end!

Experiment 1 - How does static electricity affect tap water?
You need a balloon, a plastic pen, a comb and a woollen jumper. Rub the balloon or the plastic pen hard on the jumper and then hold near to a very slow running tap. Comb your hair quickly and hold the comb near the tap. Now try rubbing a pencil on a woollen jumper and holding it by the water. What happens?

EXPERIMENT REPORT

Date: ______________________ Title: ______________________

____

Diagram

The things I used were ______________________________

____

This is what I did. ______________________________

____

____

When I held the balloon near the running tap ______________________

____

When I held the pen ______________________________

When I held the comb ______________________________

When I held the pencil ______________________________

I think the ______________________________

______________________ were charged with static electricity.

Experiment 2 - How can static electricity pick up materials?
You need a plastic pen, a woollen jumper, pepper, salt, cotton wool, pencil shavings and small cuttings of paper and cooking foil. Rub the pen on the wool and hold near to the pepper. Watch what happens. Now try the other materials. Fill in the chart below.

EXPERIMENT REPORT

Date: ________________________ Title: ________________________

____

Diagram

The things I used were ____

____

This is what I did. ____

____

____

Material	Picked up	Did not pick up
Pepper		
Salt		
Cotton wool		
Pencil shavings		
Paper cuttings		
Foil cuttings		

I found out that ____

____

Questions to answer

1) What is moving electricity called? ______

2) What is "standing still" electricity called? ______

3) Can a balloon become charged with static electricity? ______

4) How does static electricity affect slow running water? ______

5) Can static electricity attract paper? ______

6) Do you think static electricity could lift heavy objects? ______

Problems to solve

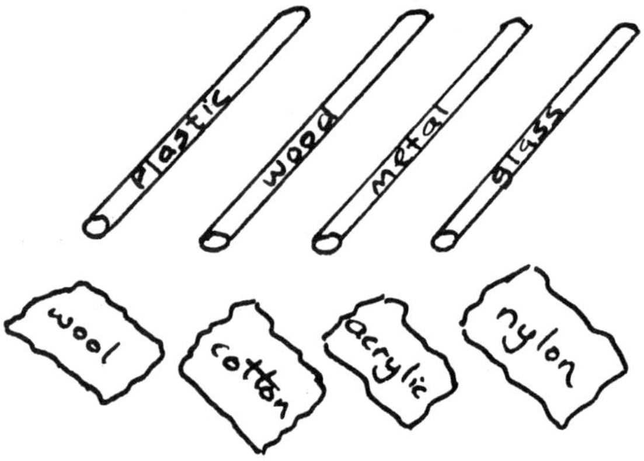

Can you make static electricity using materials other than plastic and wool?

Research the causes and effects of Thunder and Lightening.

HOW CAN YOU MAKE A SIMPLE CIRCUIT?

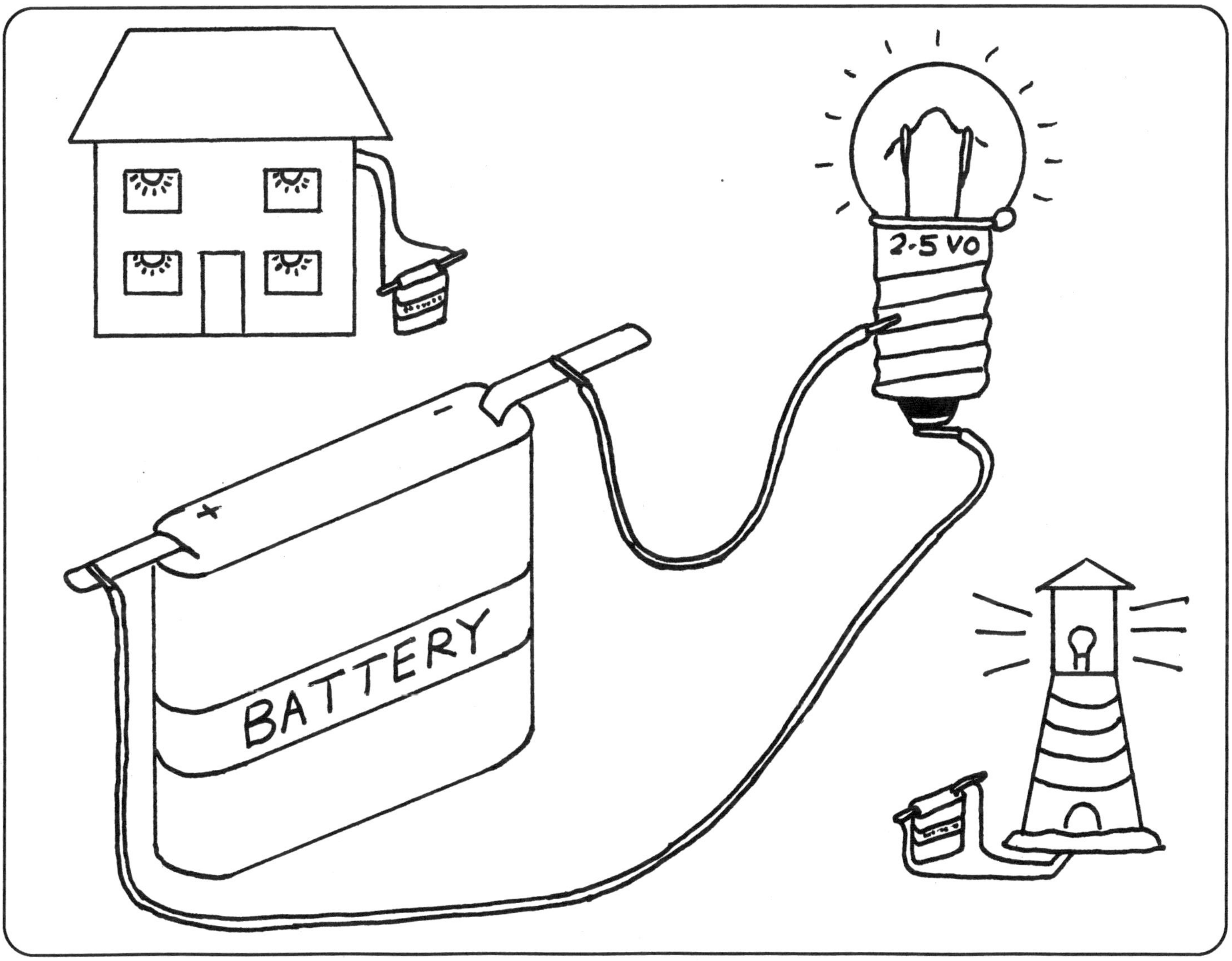

When a bulb is lit up electricity is flowing through it. To make electricity move you need a battery and some wires. If one side of the battery is connected to one part of the bulb by wire and a return wire is taken from a different part of the bulb back to the other side of the battery, a circle or circuit has been made. This will make the bulb light up.

Experiment 1 - How can you light a bulb?

You need a 4.5v battery, two wires and a torch bulb. Hold the wires tightly onto the bulb, one at the side and one underneath. Ask a friend to hold the other ends of the wires onto the metal parts of the battery. What happens?

EXPERIMENT REPORT

Date: ______________________ Title: ______________________

____

Diagram

	A large drawing of a torch bulb.

The things I used were ______________________

____

This is what I did.______________________

____

____

The bulb lit when ______________________

____

The bulb flickered when ______________________

____

If I look carefully inside the bulb I can see ______________________

____

Draw a picture of this in the space provided.

Experiment 2 - Are all bulbs the same?

You need a 4.5v battery, 2 wires with crocodile clips, a bulb holder and two torch bulbs. Screw one bulb into the holder. Make a simple circuit to light the bulb. Now try the other bulb. What happens?

EXPERIMENT REPORT

Date: ______________________ Title: ______________________

____

Diagram

The things I used were ______________________

____

This is what I did. ______________________

____

____

When I lit the bulbs I noticed ______________________

____

The crocodile clips improved the circuit because ______________________

____

The bulb holder improved the circuit because ______________________

____

Questions to answer

1) How can you tell if electricity is flowing through a bulb? ____________________

____

2) What makes electricity flow or move? ____________________

____

3) What do you need to make a simple circuit? ____________________

____

4) Do wires have to be held on tight or will slack wires do? ____________________

____

5) Are all bulbs the same? ____________________

____

6) What happens to a battery when a bulb is left on for hours? ____________________

____

Problems to solve

Can you make a model with lights that work?

Can you make two bulbs light at the same time using one battery?

HOW DOES A SWITCH WORK?

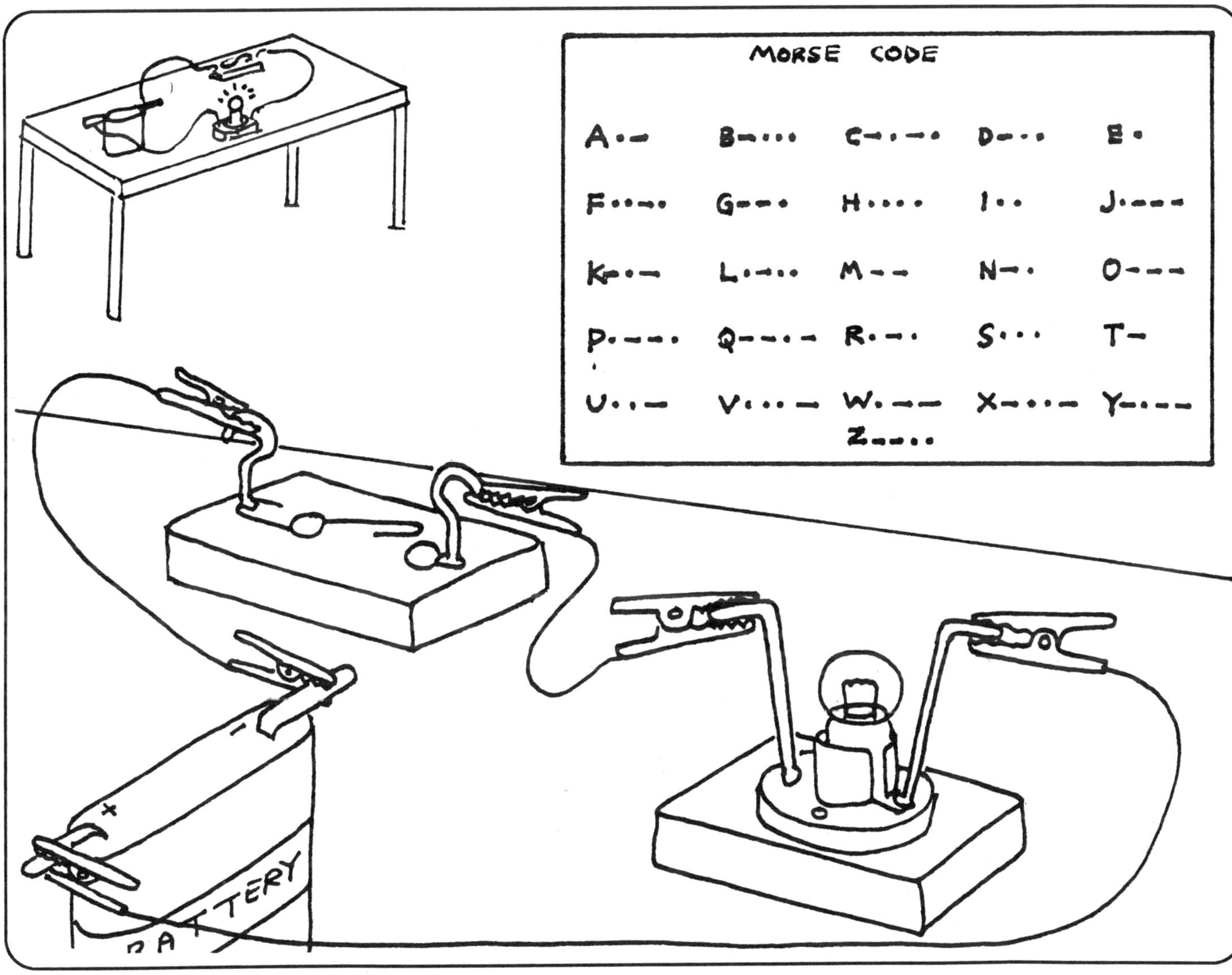

If a battery is connected to a bulb using two wires to make a circuit the bulb lights up. If we add a switch the bulb can be turned on and off. A switch makes a 'gap' in the circuit. When the gap is open the electric current <u>can not</u> flow round the circuit. The electricity can not jump across the gap. When the gap is closed the electricity flows and the light comes on.

Experiment 1 - Can you make a simple switch?

Join two wires together using crocodile clips. Now use this 'long' wire in a circuit to light a bulb from a 4.5v battery. Switch the bulb on and off by making a gap. Now try adding a simple paper clip switch into your circuit.

EXPERIMENT REPORT

Date: ______________________ Title: ______________________

____

Diagram

The things I used were ______________________________

____

This is what I did. ______________________________

____

____

The bulb was lit when ______________________________

____

____

The bulb went out when ______________________________

____

I think the bulb came on because ______________________________

____

Experiment 2 - Can messages be sent using a switch?

Make a circuit to light a bulb using a paper clip switch. Ask a friend to do the same. Use morse-code to send messages across the classroom. Is it possible?

EXPERIMENT REPORT

Date: ______________________ Title: ______________________

____

Diagram

The things I used were ______________________

____

This is what I did. ______________________

____

____

Morse code letters were sent by ______________________

____

____

We found it ______________________ to send messages in this way.

The message we sent was ______________________

____

Questions to answer

1) What would you need to make a simple circuit? ______________________________

____

2) How can you put a light on or off? ______________________________

____

3) How does a switch work? ______________________________

____

4) Can electricity from a 4.5v battery jump across a gap? ____________________

____

5) What is 'Morse Code' used for? ______________________________

____

6) Who uses 'Morse Code'? ______________________________

____

Problems to solve

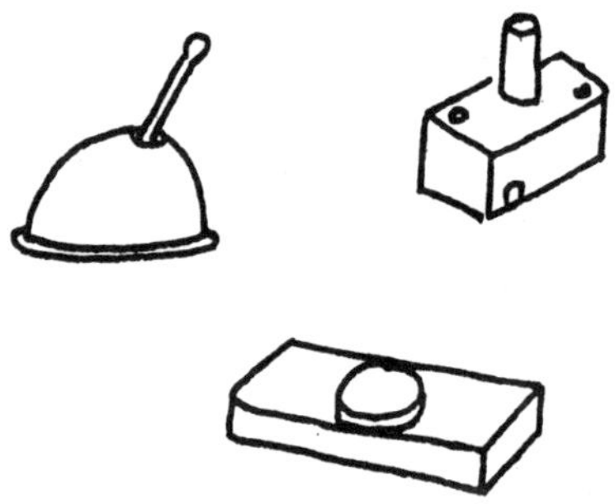

Switches come in different shapes and sizes. Try different types in a simple circuit. Investigate how they work.

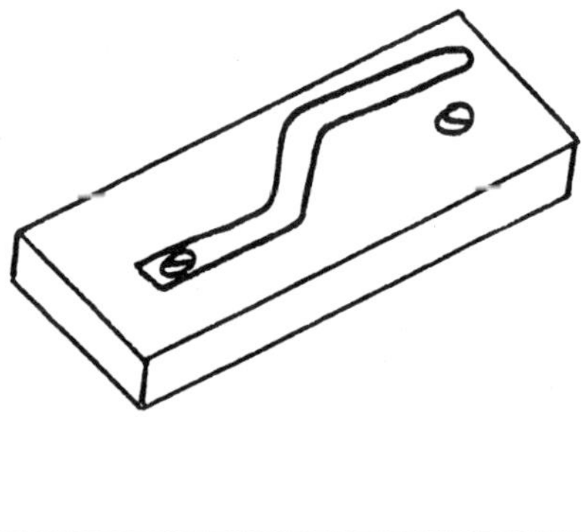

Draw and make a switch of your own design.

WHAT IS A WIRE?

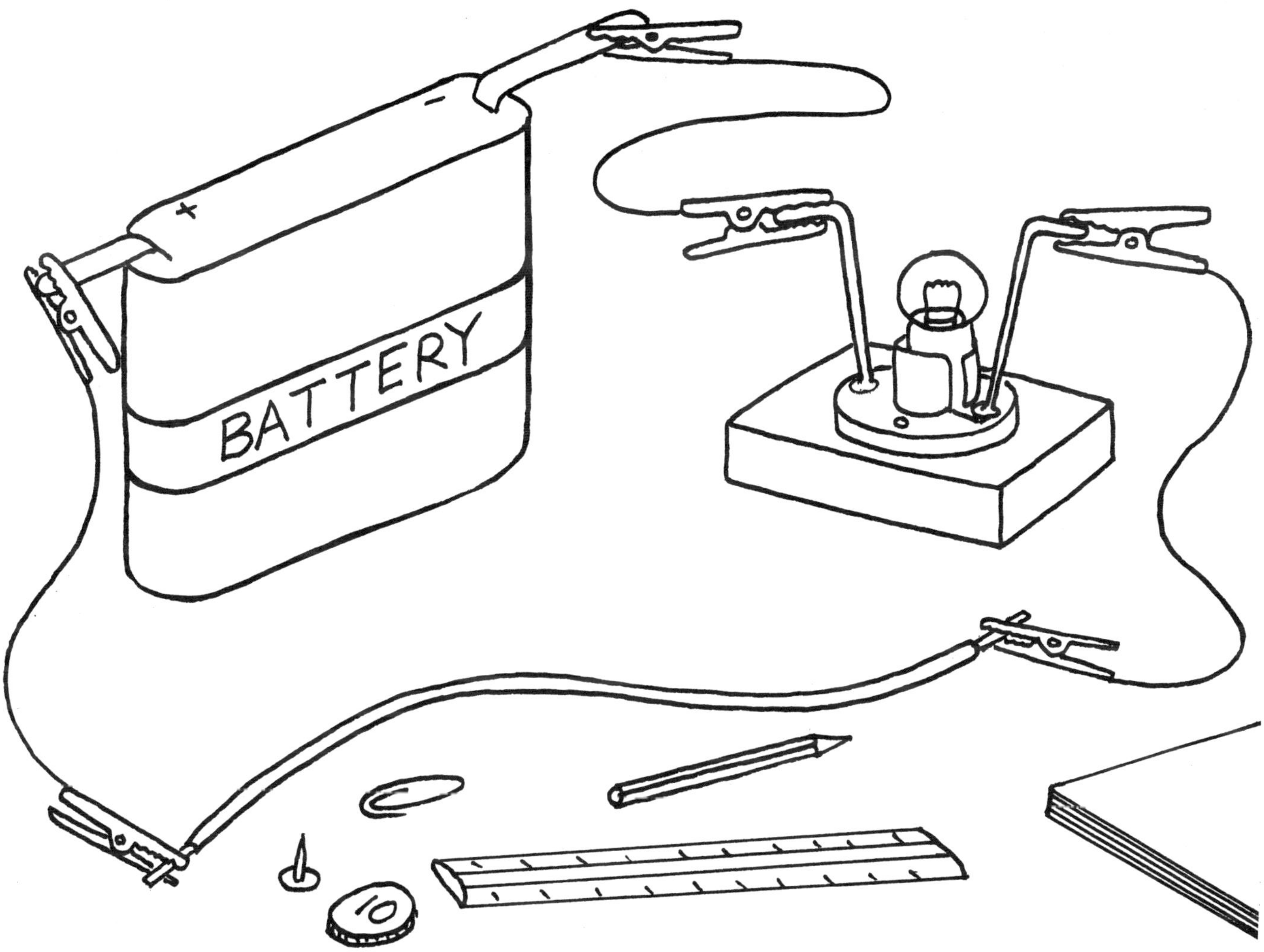

Electricity will flow or move through some materials but not others. If electricity will flow through a material we say the material is a <u>conductor</u> of electricity. If electricity will not flow through a material we say the material is an <u>insulator</u>. A wire is often made of two materials - a conductor to pass electricity on the inside - an insulator to protect people on the outside.

Experiment 1 - Which materials conduct electricity?

Find a 4.5v battery, a bulb and holder, three wires with crocodile clips and a number of small objects such as a ruler, a rubber, a paper clip, a drawing pin etc. Make a circuit which makes electricity pass through one object. Does the bulb light? Try the other objects. Fill in the table.

EXPERIMENT REPORT

Date: ______________________ Title: ______________________

____

Diagram

The things I used were ______________________________

____

This is what I did. ______________________________

____

Object	Passed electricity through = Conductor	Did not pass electricity = Insulator

I think all of the conductors were made of ______________________

Experiment 2 - Which parts of a wire conduct electricity?

Find a 4.5v battery, a bulb and holder, three wires with crocodile clips and a plastic wire with bare metal ends. Make a simple circuit and test the bulb. Now include the plastic wire with bare metal ends in the circuit. What happens?

EXPERIMENT REPORT

Date: ______________________ Title: ______________________

____

Diagram

The things I used were ______________________________

____

This is what I did. ______________________________

____

____

With the crocodile clips fastened to the bare metal ends of the wire the bulb __________

____

With the crocodile clips fastened to the plastic cover on the wire the bulb __________

____

With one clip on a metal end and the other clip on the plastic cover the bulb __________

____

The wire only conducts when ______________________________

____

Questions to answer

1) Will electricity pass through all materials? ______________________

____

2) What is a conductor? ______________________

____

3) What is an insulator? ______________________

____

4) How did you know if electricity was flowing in your circuit? ______________________

____

5) What is a wire? ______________________

____

6) Why does a mains wire usually have a plastic cover? ______________________

____

Problems to solve

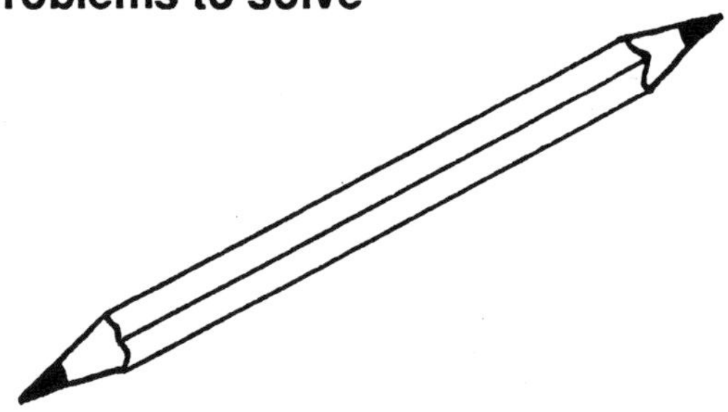

Will electricity pass through the lead in the centre of a pencil?

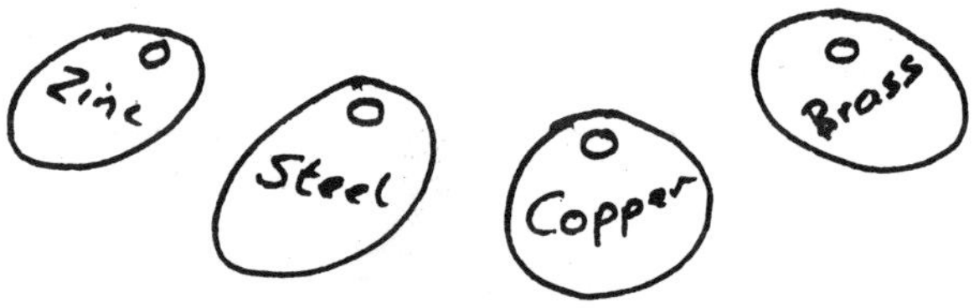

Are all metals good conductors of electricity?

HOW CAN ELECTRICITY HELP US? (PART 1)

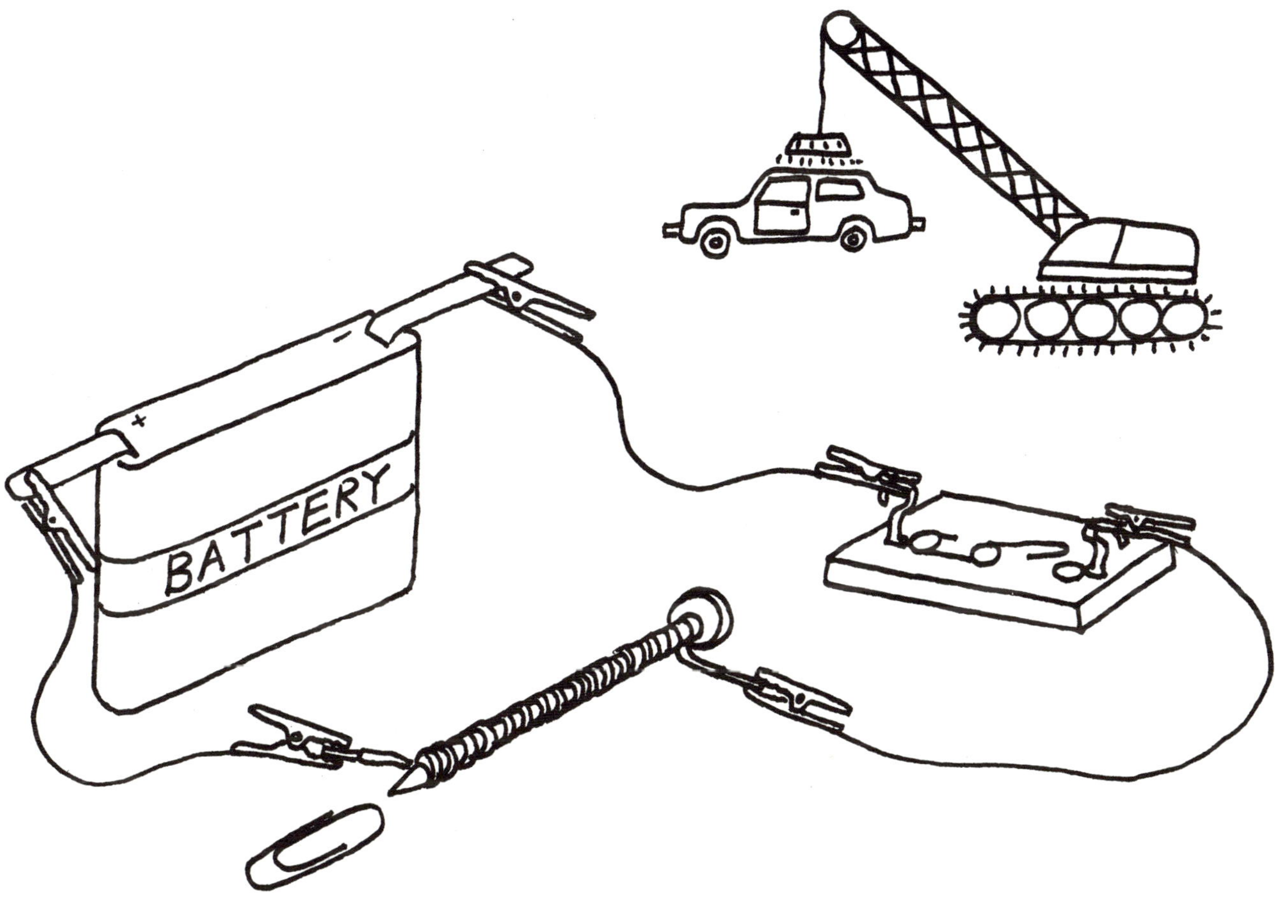

Magnets pick up some metal objects because they have an 'invisible' magnetic field. A wire has a very tiny magnetic field round it when electricity goes through it. If we wind lots of turns of wire round a nail we can make an electric magnet. Electric magnets are used on cranes in factories for lifting heavy metal things. They are also used to power small electrical devices in the home such as electric buzzers or electric bells.

Experiment 1 - Can you make an electric magnet?

You need a 4.5v battery, a paper clip switch, three wires with crocodile clips, an 8cm nail and 1m of fine plastic coated wire. Check the nail does not act like a magnet. Wrap the wire tightly round the nail. Make the circuit shown on page 1. Hold the nail close to a paper clip and press the switch. What happens?

EXPERIMENT REPORT

Date: ______________________ Title: ______________________

____

Diagram

Equipment needed: ______________________________

____

Method used: ___________________________________

____

____

Observations made: ______________________________

____

____

How many paper clips will your electric magnet lift? ______________

____

____

Experiment 2 - Can you make a buzzer or bell ring?

You need a 4.5v battery, a push button switch, four wires with clips, a buzzer, a bell, a copper washer and a bent coat hanger on a wooden base. Make a circuit with a battery, bell and switch. Make a circuit with battery, buzzer and switch. Include the wire coat hanger in one circuit. Can you make a game of skill?

EXPERIMENT REPORT

Date: ______________________ Title: ______________________

____

Diagram

Equipment needed: ____

____

____

Methods used: ____

____

____

Observations made: ____

____

____

How did you make a game of skill? ____

____

____

Questions to answer

1) Why do magnets pick up metal objects? ______________________________

____

2) When does a wire have a magnetic field? ______________________________

____

3) How can you make an electric magnet? ______________________________

____

4) When does an electric magnet attract metal objects? ______________________

____

5) What are buzzers and bells used for in the home? ______________________

____

6) What makes an electric buzzer or bell operate? ______________________

____

Problems to solve

How powerful can you make a home made electric magnet?

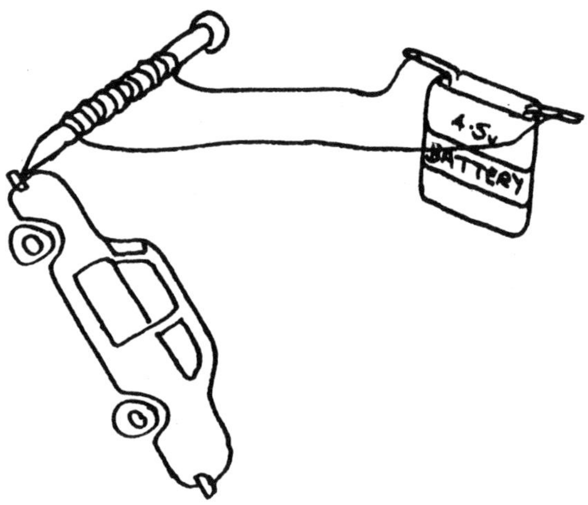

Design and build a burglar alarm which sets off a bell or buzzer.

HOW CAN ELECTRICITY HELP US? (PART 2)

An electric heater is a small fire powered by electricity. An electric motor is a small engine powered by electricity. A lady was drying her hair when the hairdryer broke down. She removed the plug from the wall socket and looked inside the dryer. She found the hairdryer used an electric heater to make hot air and an electric motor to blow it out.

Experiment 1 - Can you make a wire hot?

You need a 4.5v battery, two wires with clips, a plate and some wire wool. Remove 1 strand only from the wire wool and place on the plate. Connect the wires to the battery and use them to touch the wire wool. Try long lengths and short lengths of wire wool. What happens?

EXPERIMENT REPORT

Date: ______________________ Title: ______________________

____

Diagram

Equipment needed: ______________________________

____

Method used: __________________________________

____

____

Observations made: ______________________________

____

____

What was the greatest length of wire wool to heat up? ______________

____

____

Experiment 2 - Can you make an electric motor run?

You need a 4.5v battery, two wires, a small electric motor, some blue tack and a circle of card. Draw a pattern on the card and fasten it using blue tack to the axle on the motor. Connect the motor to the battery. What happens?

EXPERIMENT REPORT

Date: ______________________ Title: ______________________

____

Diagram

Equipment needed: ______________________________

____

Method used: ___________________________________

____

____

Observations made: ______________________________

____

____

What happens when you reverse the wires on the battery? ______________

____

____

Questions to answer

1) What is an electric heater? ______________________________

____

2) How are electric heaters used in the home? ______________________________

____

3) What is an electric motor? ______________________________

____

4) Which machines in the home use electric motors? ______________________________

____

5) How do you make a very thin wire hot? ______________________________

____

6) How do you make an electric motor change direction? ______________________________

____

Problems to solve

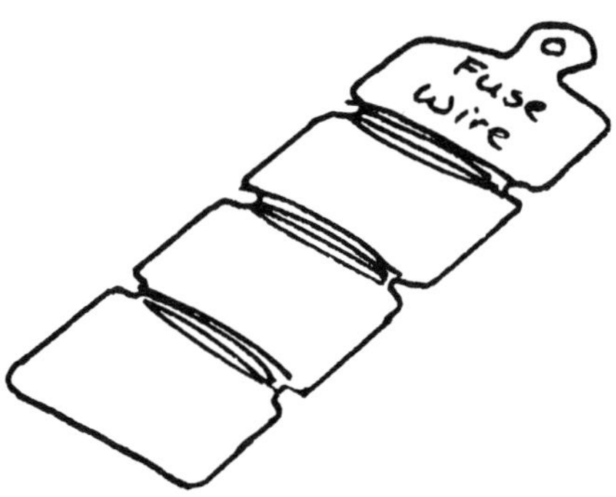

Research what fuses are, how they work and what they are used for.

Design and make a simple lifting device using an electric motor. How much will it lift?

HOW CAN SWITCHES CONTROL ELECTRICAL DEVICES?

Nearly everyday you go into your house and 'switch' on a light or 'switch' on the television. One switch in the circuit is enough to do this. Sometimes we want to do more complex actions such as operate two bulbs separately from each other or reverse the direction of an electric motor. To do this we need to use a number of simple switches together or we may use a more complicated switch such as a double-pole-double-throw switch.

Experiment 1 - Can you make a simple traffic light?

You need a 4.5v battery, two paper-clip switches, two bulbs in holders, 6 wires with clips and red and green tissue paper. Cover the bulbs with tissue. Connect up the wires as shown in the picture below. Can you operate a traffic light?

EXPERIMENT REPORT

Date: ______________________ Title: ______________________

____

Diagram

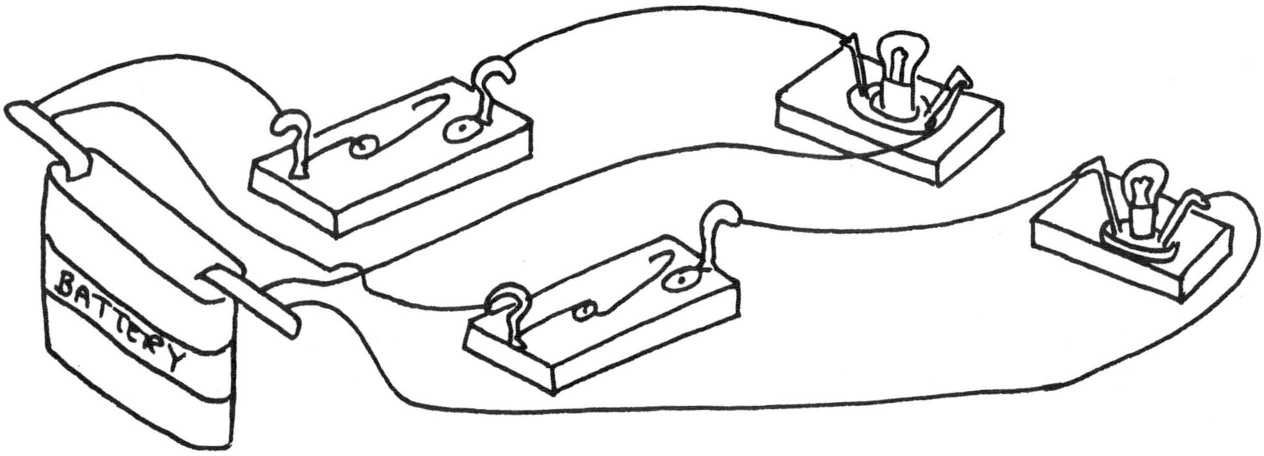

Equipment needed: ____

____

Method used: ____

____

____

Observations made: ____

____

____

Use toy cars to act out a road works scene. What problems do you have? ______________

____

____

Experiment 2 - Can you make an electric motor change direction?

You need a 4.5v battery, four paper-clip switches, an electric motor, and 8 wires with clips. Connect the wires as shown in the picture below. Which switches make the motor work?

EXPERIMENT REPORT

Date: ______________________ Title: ______________________

____

Diagram

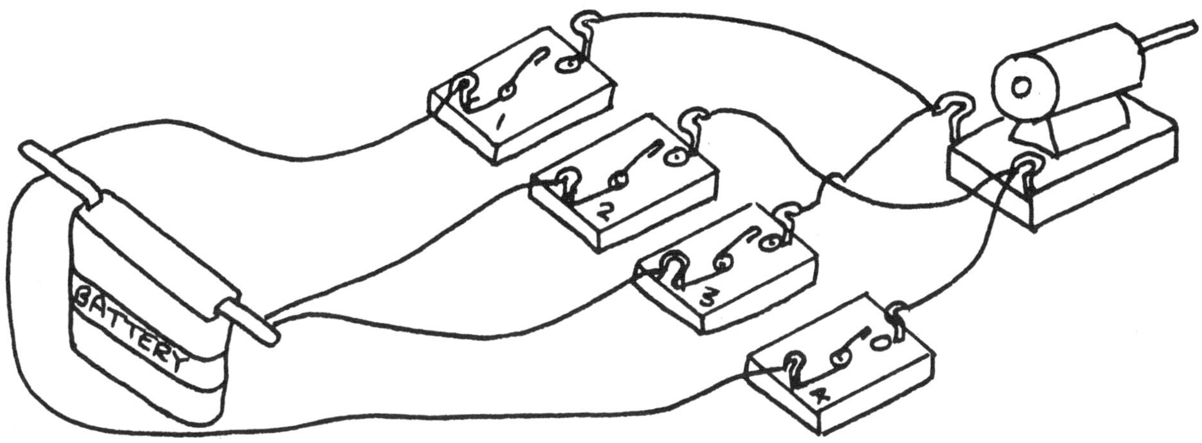

Equipment needed: ____

____

Method used: ____

____

____

Switch (1) and (2) pressed = ____________

Switch (1) and (3) pressed = ____________

Switch (1) and (4) pressed = ____________

Switch (2) and (3) pressed = ____________

Switch (2) and (4) pressed = ____________

Switch (3) and (4) pressed = ____________

Which switches made the motor turn clockwise? ______________________

____

Which switches made the motor turn anti-clockwise? ______________________

____

Questions to answer

1) What may you use a switch for in the home? ______________________

____

2) How does a switch work? ______________________

____

3) Why might you need to use more than one switch? ______________________

____

____

4) How many switches did you need to operate your traffic light? ______________________

____

5) How many switches did you need to reverse the electric motor? ______________________

____

6) What jobs do some switches in a real car do? ______________________

____

Problems to solve

Can you design a traffic light which will run the correct sequence of Red, Amber and Green?

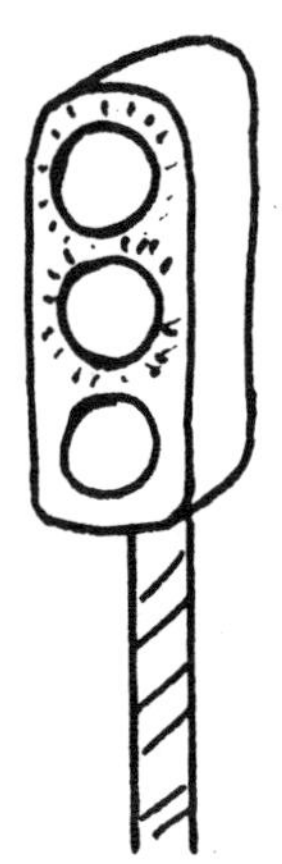

Design and build a railway crossing barrier which is operated by an electric motor.

WHAT ARE LOGIC GATES?

A gate in a circuit can be another name for a switch. An AND GATE in a circuit needs one switch AND another to be closed before the current will flow. An OR GATE gives a choice of one switch OR another switch to be closed before the circuit is complete. A NOT GATE requires one switch to be closed but NOT the other switch before the circuit will operate. By using logic these gates can be used to operate complex machinery such as computers or more simple devices such as a burglar alarm.

Experiment 1 - Can you construct an AND GATE circuit?

You need a 4.5v battery, a push button switch, a paper clip switch, a buzzer and four wires with clips. Make up the circuit shown below. When does the burglar alarm buzzer sound? (N.B. the buzzer must be connected in the correct way).

EXPERIMENT REPORT

Date: ______________________ Title: ______________________

____

Diagram

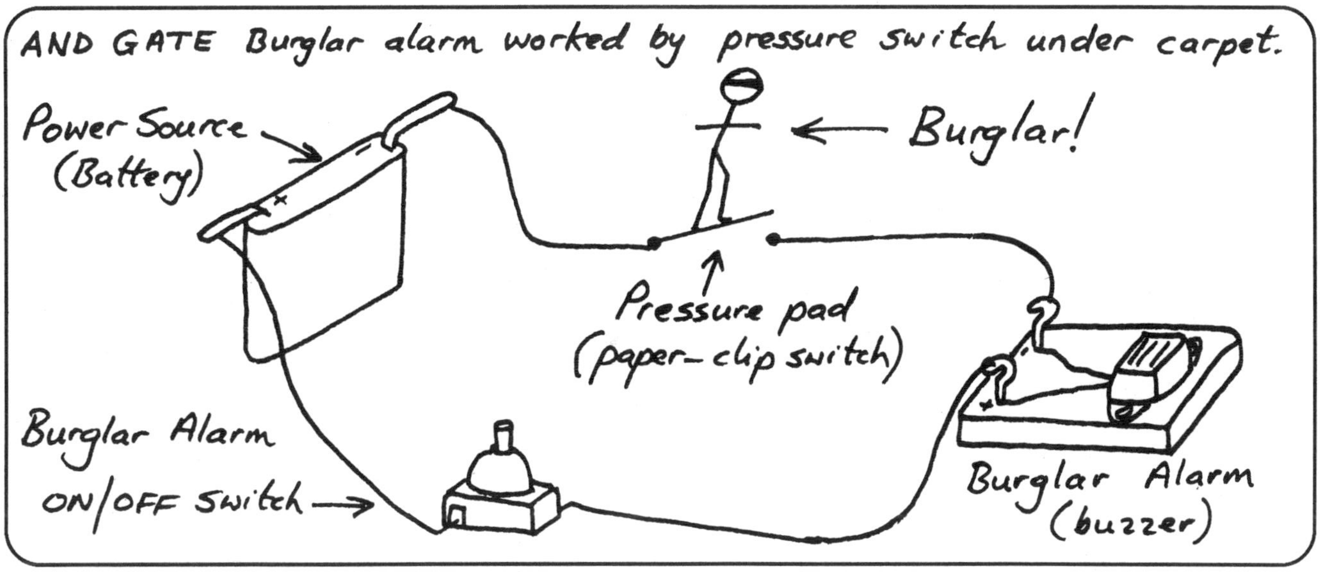

Equipment needed: ____

____

____

Method used: ____

____

____

Observations made: ____

____

____

The burglar alarm will only light up when ______________________

AND ____

Experiment 2 - Can you construct a NOT GATE circuit?

You need a 4.5v battery, a bulb in holder, a push button switch, a paper clip switch, a buzzer and six wires with clips. Make up the circuit shown below. Hold the paper clip switch down (this would be the window closed) and switch on the circuit. What happens? How can the alarm be set off? (N.B. The buzzer must be connected in the correct way).

EXPERIMENT REPORT

Date: ______________________ Title: ______________________

____

Diagram

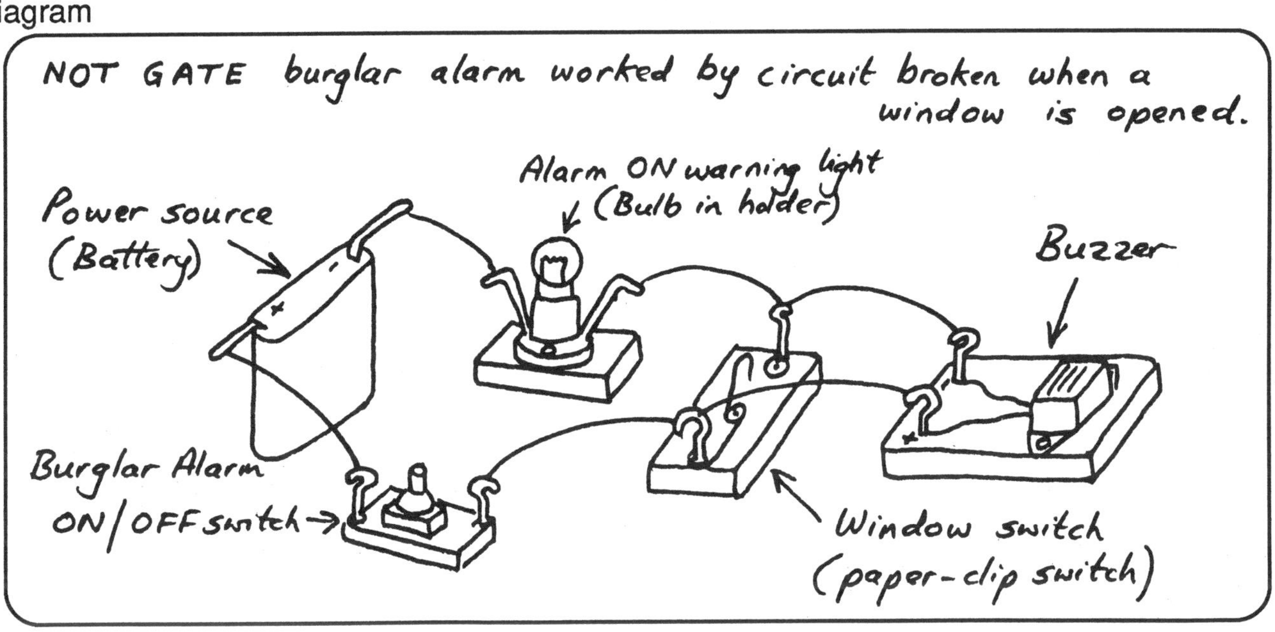

Equipment needed: ____

____

Method used: ____

____

How do you know when the circuit is switched on? ______________________

____

____

When the paper clip switch was held down (in real life the window switch closed) and the circuit was switched on ______________________

____

When the paper clip switch was opened (in real life the window opened) and the circuit was switched on ______________________

____

Questions to answer

1) What is a gate in a circuit? ______________________________

____

2) When does electricity flow in an AND GATE circuit? ______________________________

____

3) When does electricity flow in an OR GATE circuit? ______________________________

____

4) When does electricity flow in a NOT GATE circuit? ______________________________

____

5) What can these circuits be used for? ______________________________

____

6) What is logic? ______________________________

____

Problems to solve

Can you make a logic game which lights a bulb through three push button switches?

Can you make a burglar alarm circuit which has a pressure pad OR a window switch to set off the alarm?

CAN YOU CONSTRUCT A CIRCUIT FROM A PLAN?

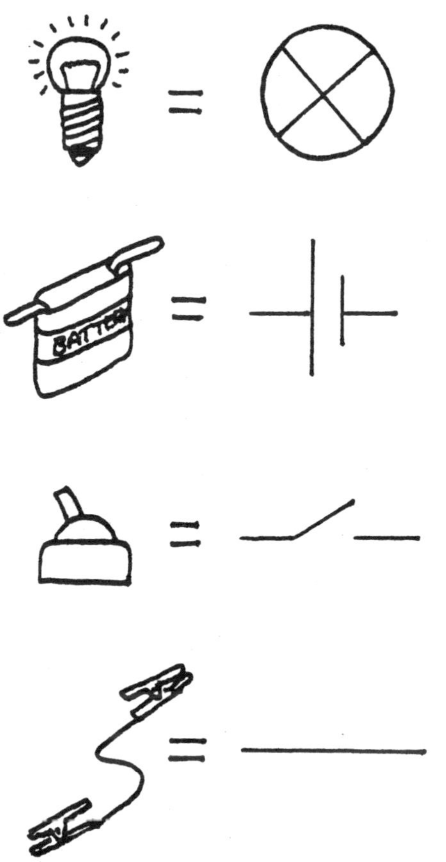

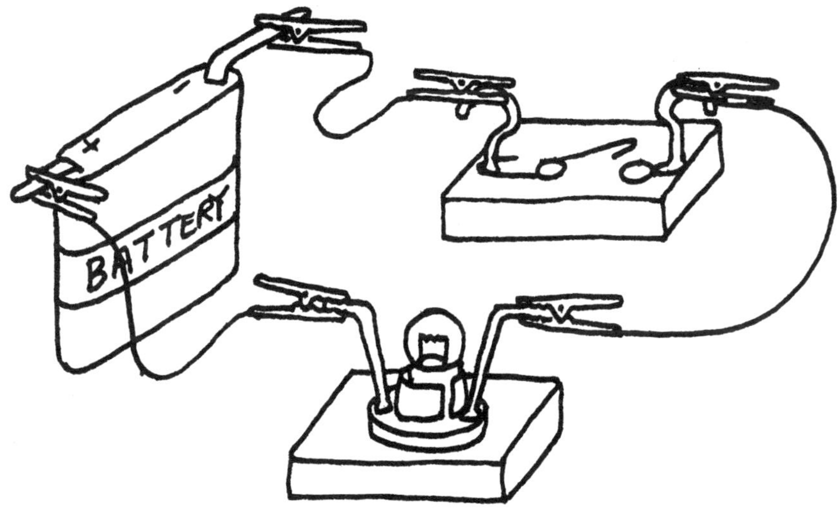

This circuit is drawn as :

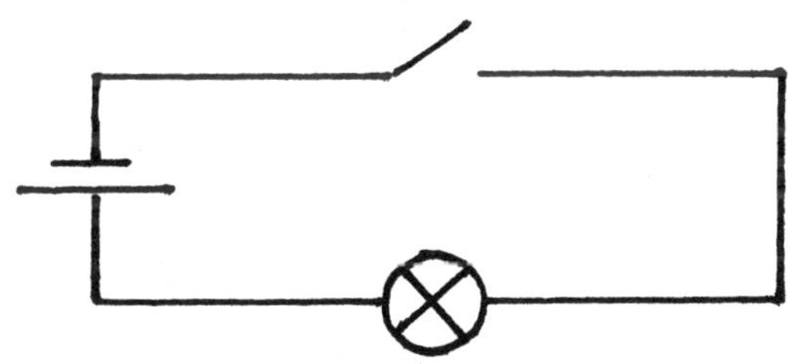

When an electrician is wiring a car or a house she/he may use hundreds of different wires and components. To get the connections in the correct places the electrician follows a drawing. Hundreds of sketches of light bulbs and switches would take a lot of space and could be very confusing so signs and symbols are used instead. In this way a large amount of information can be contained in a small wiring diagram.

Some circuits are connected in "series". Some circuits are connected in "parallel". You can use wiring diagrams to construct "series" or "parallel" circuits.

Experiment 1 - Can you construct a "Series" circuit from a plan?

You need a 4.5v battery, two bulbs in holders and three wires with crocodile clips. Construct this circuit.

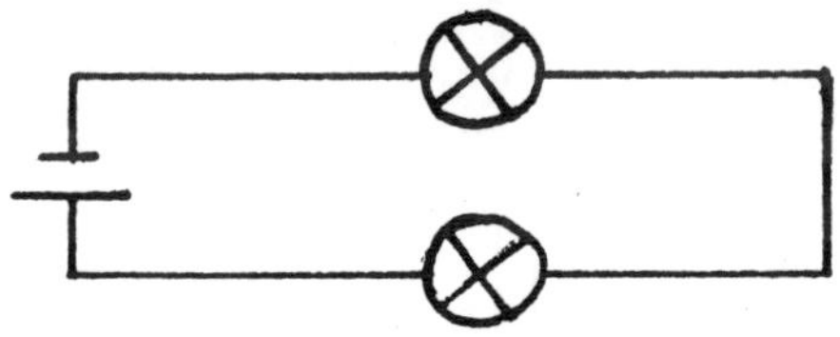

EXPERIMENT REPORT

Date: ______________________ Title: ______________________

____

Diagram

Equipment needed: ____

____

____

Method used: ____

____

____

Observations made: ____

____

____

Make a circuit with only one bulb connected. Which circuit had the brightest lights? Why?

____

____

Experiment 2 - Can you construct a "Parallel" circuit from a plan?

You need a 4.5v battery, two bulbs in holders and four wires with clips. Construct this circuit.

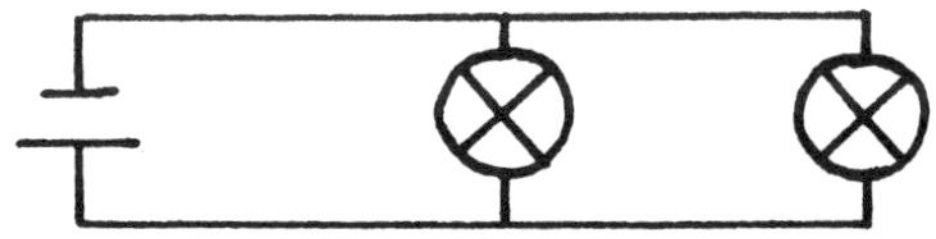

EXPERIMENT REPORT

Date: ______________________ Title: ______________________

____

Diagram

Equipment needed: ____

____

____

Method used: ____

____

____

Observations made: ____

____

____

Make a circuit with only one bulb connected. Which circuit had the brightest lights? Why?

____

____

Questions to answer

1) What is an electrician? ______________________________

____

2) How do electricians know where to put wires? ______________________________

____

3) Why are drawings not used on wiring diagrams? ______________________________

____

4) How are bulbs wired in "series"? ______________________________

____

____

5) How are bulbs wired in "parallel"? ______________________________

____

____

6) Which circuit do you think would run the battery down most quickly? ______________

____

Problems to solve

Can you construct "series" and "parallel" circuits with three bulbs?

Can you design wiring diagrams of "series" and "parallel" circuits with four bulbs?

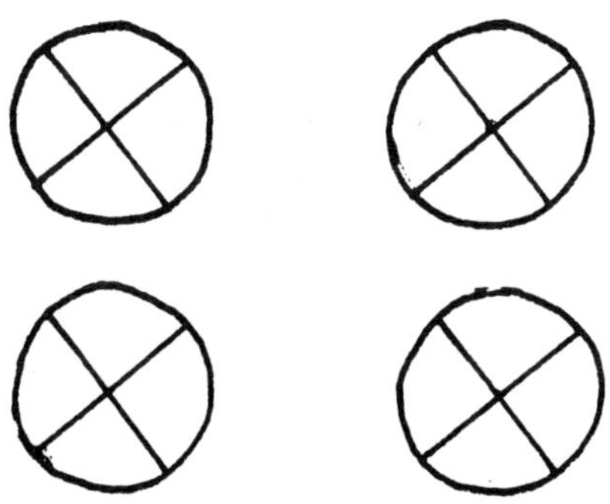

CAN YOU VARY THE FLOW OF ELECTRICITY IN A CIRCUIT?

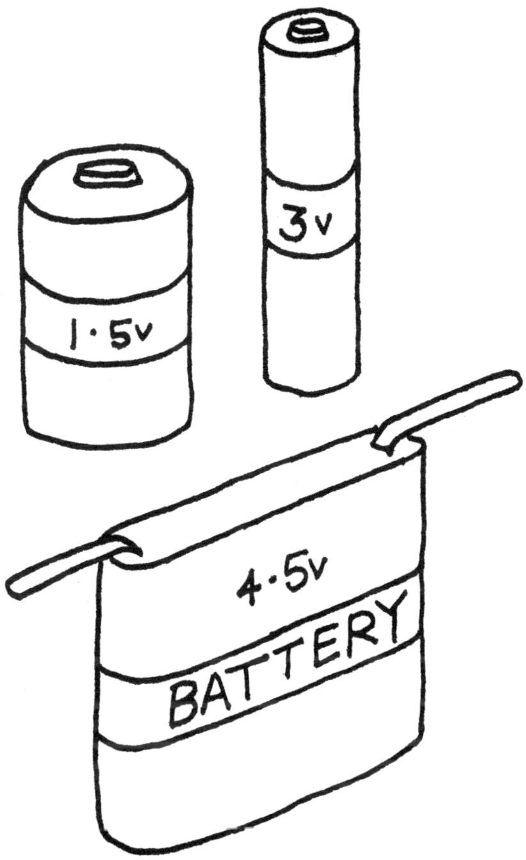

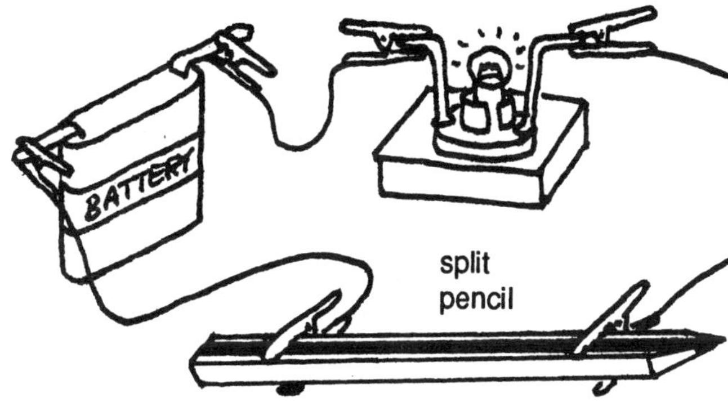

This circuit is drawn as :

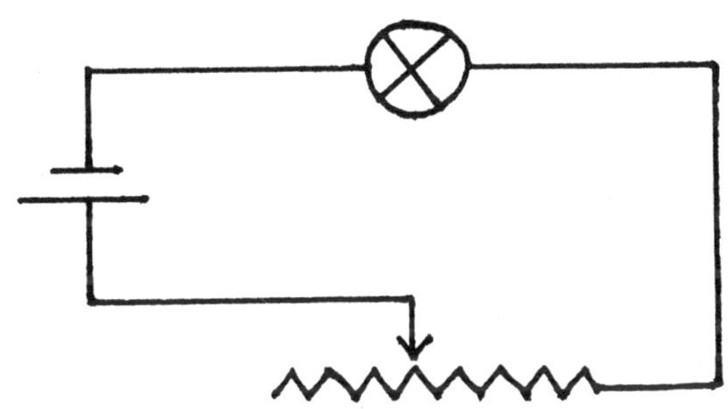

Batteries come in various shapes and sizes - some are big, some are small, some are powerful and some are not. A battery "pushes" electric current round a circuit. The number of volts maked on the battery tells you how much "push" a battery can give. Different batteries create different flows of electricity in a circuit.

Metals are good conductors of electricity. Plastics are good insulators. Some materials conduct electricity a little. These are called partial conductors. The material in the centre of a pencil is a partial conductor of electricity. Partial conductors can also be used to vary the flow of electricity in a circuit.

Experiment 1 - How do different sized batteries affect a simple circuit?

You need a 1.5v, a 3v and a 4.5v battery, two wires, a bulb and holder. Construct these circuits in turn. Compare the results.

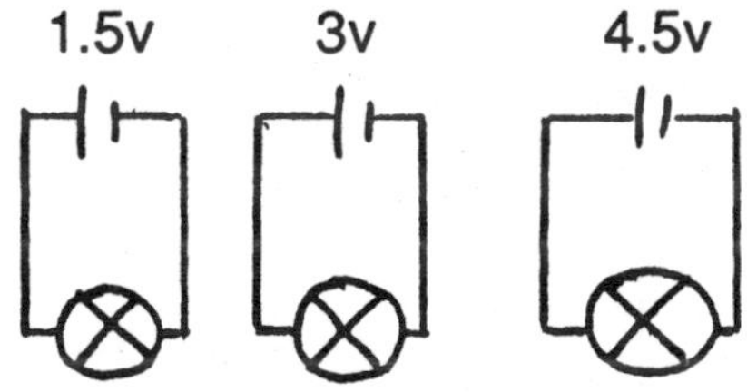

EXPERIMENT REPORT

Date: ______________________ Title: ______________________

____

Diagram

Equipment needed: ____

____

____

Method used: ____

____

____

Observations made: ____

____

____

Would your test be fair if one battery was near the end of its useful life? ______________

____

Experiment 2 - How does a partial conductor affect a simple circuit?

You need a 4.5v battery, a bulb and holder, three wires with clips and a pencil split to expose the centre. Construct this circuit. Move the clips along the pencil. What happens?

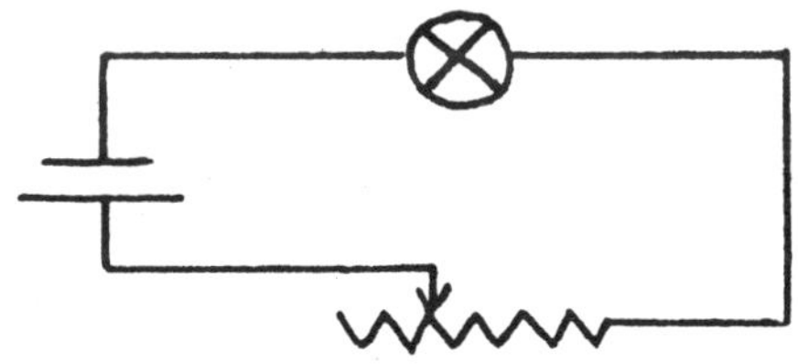

EXPERIMENT REPORT

Date: ______________________ Title: ______________________

____

Diagram

Equipment needed: ____

____

Method used: ____

____

Observations made: ____

____

____

When was the bulb the brightest? ____

____

When was the bulb the dullest? ____

____

Questions to answer

1) How do batteries differ? ____

____

2) What does a battery do?____

____

3) What do 'volts' tell us? ____

____

4) What is a partial conductor? ____

____

5) How can a split pencil be used to vary the flow of electricity in a simple circuit? ______

____

____

6) How do you know the flow of electricity is varied? ___________________________

____

Problems to solve

What happens if more than one battery is used in a circuit?

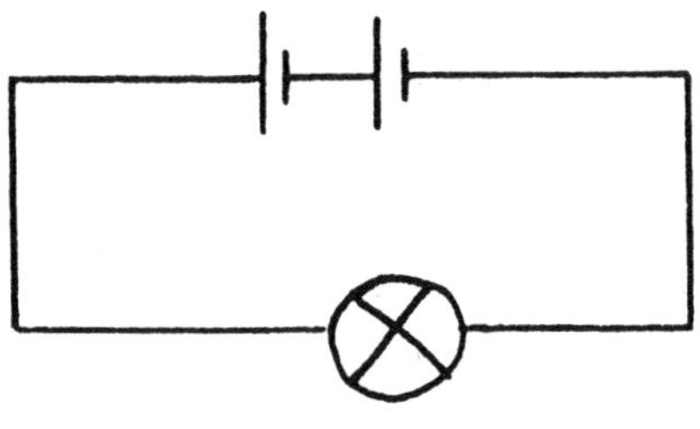

Do some pencils conduct electricity better than others?

Level 2 - WHAT IS A MAGNET? - Teacher's Notes

Equipment needed: 10 small objects (e.g. rubber, paper clip, pencil sharpener, drawing pin, safety pin, scissors etc.), 2 bar magnets in good condition (your local Secondary School or Teacher's Centre could re-magnetize your old bar magnets), an all steel horse-shoe shaped magnet, again in good condition, a large box of paper clips and a direction compass.

Experiment 1: Aim - to help children understand that some materials are attracted to magnets and others are not.

It is important that the teacher ensures the collection of objects contains at least some objects which are attracted to the magnet. The children may need help when discussing the type of materials attracted to the magnet.

The children should be encouraged to experiment with the two bar magnets, held end to end. By doing this they will experience the magnetic forces of attraction and repulsion. The term magnetic poles (the ends) may be introduced here. There are two types, the NORTH POLE and the SOUTH POLE. Like poles repel. Unlike poles attract. The South Pole on a direction compass points North.

Experiment 2: Aim - to help the children to understand that some parts of a magnet have a stronger attraction than others.

The bar magnet and the horse-shoe magnet should be used in turn to see how many paper clips they can lift. It will be found that the ends of the bar magnet will lift many more paper clips than the centre part.

A horse-shoe magnet is merely a bar magnet which has been bent into a horse-shoe shape. If the two magnets used were of equal strength, and in equally good condition it would be found that the horse-shoe magnet could lift more than the bar magnet.

Questions to answer

The children will probably know that magnets are used in some simple toys e.g. magnetic fishing game. Other uses could include direction compass and some simple door catches.

Problems to solve

This extension activity is for those children who would like to explore further the properties of magnetism. Great consideration needs to be given as to what is a fair test in their investigations.

Experiment 1 - Which things are attracted to magnets?

Find 10 small objects. Hold a bar magnet near each one in turn. Write in the space below which are pulled by the magnet and which are not. Now start your report.

Date: *Monday 15th October*

Title: *Things that are attracted to magnets*

Picture of what you did

I needed *a bar magnet and ten small objects.*

Things pulled by the magnet	Things not pulled by the magnet
paper clip	*rubber*
drawing pin	*ruler*
staple	*pencil*
pencil sharpener	*pen*
	book
	desk

I think the things pulled by the magnet were made of *iron or steel metals.*

If a bar magnet is held near another bar magnet *sometimes they stick together and sometimes they push apart.*

Experiment 2 - Which is the strongest part of a magnet?

Find a bar magnet, a horseshoe magnet and a large box of paper clips. Count how many paper clips are lifted by different parts of each magnet. Start your report.

Date: *Tuesday 16th October*

Title: *A test to find the strongest part of a magnet*

Picture of what you did

I needed *two magnets and many paper clips.*

One end of the bar magnet lifted *nine paper clips.*

The opposite end of the bar magnet lifted *twelve paper clips.*

The middle of the bar magnet lifted *one paper clip.*

The ends of the horseshoe magnet lifted *twenty paper clips.*

The curved part of the horseshoe magnet lifted *no paper clips.*

I think the strongest parts of a magnet are *the ends because the ends attracted most of the paper clips.*

Questions to answer

1) What is a magnet? *A magnet is a piece of metal which will pull other pieces of metal towards itself.*

2) Is a magnet sticky to touch? *A magnet is not sticky.*

3) Can you see magnetism? *You cannot see magnetism*

4) What does the word attract mean? *Attract means pull towards.*

5) What is the name given to the strongest part of a magnet? *The strongest part of the magnet is the end, called the pole.*

6) Name some jobs a magnet could be used for. *A magnet can be used for lifting things and playing with. It is also used in electric bells, electric buzzers and electric motors.*

Problems to solve

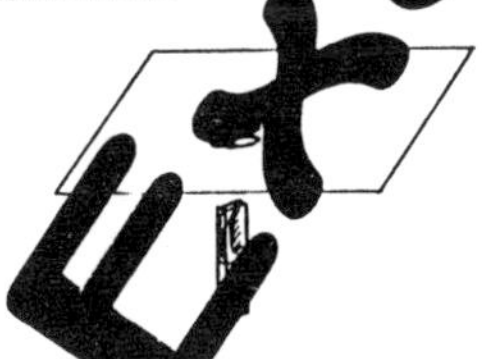

Can magnets work through materials such as paper or card?

How does a magnet effect a direction compass? Why?

Are all magnets the same strength?

Level 2 - IS ELECTRICITY SAFE? - Teacher's Notes

Equipment needed: Some simple children's reference books which show uses of electricity in the home.

Find Out - What is Electricity used for in your home? Aim - to help the children begin to think about how many everyday home-appliances depend on electricity for their source of power and how different our lives would be without these appliances.

A useful starting off point could be for the teacher to demonstrate one or two appliances (e.g. iron, hair-dryer) in the classroom. The point should be made that each device is "useless" until it is powered by electricity when it becomes a most valuable resource for us. The Electricity Council produce a number of resources which could be useful here.

Electricity Safety Quiz : Aim - to make children aware of the obvious dangers of mains electricity and teach them to treat electrical equipment in a sensible and safe way.

The filling in of the quiz sheet could be the final activity following class discussion and/or watching an electricity board safety video, or taking part in a home-safety quiz.

Great emphasis should be made on the dangers of handling mains electrical equipment with wet hands, using equipment with broken plugs or frayed wires, and playing near electricity substations or overhead wires. The single - most important point is in general torch-type batteries are perfectly safe to handle, whereas mains electricity is LETHAL.

Electricity Poster - By asking the children to design their own poster warning of the dangers of electricity, they will be required to think about the dangers previously discussed and brought out in the Safety Quiz. The dangers can be again highlighted by discussing the points brought out in individual posters.

Find Out - What is electricity used for in your home?

Write the names of 10 things which use electricity at home. Draw a small picture of each one. Write a sentence about the job each one does.

Name	Picture	
light		A light is [illegible] for lighting [illegible]n.
television		A te[illegible]sion is used for [illegible]ing pictures.
video		A video is used for recording programmes.
fridge		A fridge is used for keeping food fresh.
washing machine		A washing machine is used for cleaning clothes.
hair dryer		A hair dryer is used for drying your hair.
radio		A radio is used for listening to music.
coo[illegible]		A cooker is used for cooking food.
iron	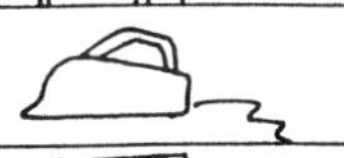	An iron is used for pressing clothes.
C.D. player		A C.D. Player is used for playing music.

Electricity Safety Quiz

Is it safe to		Ans[illegible]er [illegible]s or No
	Switch on a light with wet hands?	[illegible]
	Play with a torch battery?	Yes
	Let a baby play near an electric fire?	No
	Push in a plug with wet hands?	No
	Poke things into a wall socket?	No
	Play with a battery powered toy [illegible]r?	Yes
	Fly a kite near overhead w[illegible]s?	No
	Use an iron with damage[illegible]?	No
	Stand an electric [illegible] puddle?	No
	Touch the m[illegible] p[illegible]s o[illegible] plug when it is plugged into a [illegible]ket?	No
	Switch o[illegible] [illegible]ic light?	Yes
	Us[illegible]ked or broken plug?	No
	Play with a model railway or racing car set?	Yes
	Pla[illegible]otball near overhead wires or by an el[illegible]icity sub-station?	No

Use the next page to make up your own poster to warn people of the dangers of electricity.

BEWARE

ELECTRICITY CAN

Level 3 - CAN ELECTRICITY STAND STILL? - Teacher's Notes

Equipment needed: A balloon, a plastic pen, a comb, a woollen jumper, a pencil, pepper, salt, cotton wool, pencil shavings, small cuttings of paper and cooking foil.

Experiment 1: Aim - to help children to experience the effects of static electricity by observing the effect it has on slow-running tap water.

The balloon needs to be blown up and rubbed on a woollen jumper (synthetic materials do not have the same effect). The tap needs to be turned down to the slowest continuous stream that can be achieved for the best results. Holding the charged balloon near the stream of water attracts the stream of water towards the charged balloon. For the best results in any experiment on static electricity all of the equipment needs to be kept perfectly dry.

The comb on hair creates a similar effect. The pencil cannot be charged and therefore does not attract.

Note : The term "diagram" is introduced here. It may be necessary to talk about its meaning.

Experiment 2: Aim - to help children understand that static electricity can attract small light particles of most materials. It will be necessary to have prepared containers of the materials ready for use. (The dangers to the eyes with misuse of salt and pepper should be pointed out to the children). Each material should be tested in turn. After each test the plastic pen should be cleaned with a dry rag. It will be found that static electricity will attract all of these materials provided they are small enough and light enough to be lifted by the weak force.

Questions to answer

By doing the experiments it will become apparent that static electricity is generally a very weak force and will only attract materials such as paper when they are cut into very small pieces.

Problems to solve

This extension activity is for children who would like to investigate other ways of making static electricity.

Children may use secondary sources to research the causes of lightening.

Experiment 1 - How does static electricity affect tap water?
You need a balloon, a plastic pen, a comb and a woollen jumper. Rub the balloon or the plastic pen hard on the jumper and then hold near to a very slow running tap. Comb your hair quickly and hold the comb near the tap. Now try rubbing a pencil on a woollen jumper. What happens?

EXPERIMENT REPORT

Date: *12th December* Title: *Static electrici[illegible]nd t[illegible]er*

Diagram

The things I used were *a balloon, [illegible]ic pen, a comb, a woollen jumper and a running tap.*

This is what I did *I rubbed the [illegible] on the jumper and held it near the running tap. Then I t[illegible] the pen, the comb and the pencil.*

When I held t[illegible] balloon n[illegible]he running tap *the water moved towards the balloon.*

When [illegible] pen *t[illegible]ame happened.*

When I he[illegible] *the same happened.*

When I held the pencil *nothing happened.*

I think the *balloon, the pen and the comb* were charged with static electricity.

Experiment 2 - How can static electricity pick up materials?
You need a plastic pen, a woollen jumper, pepper, salt, cotton wool, pencil shavings and small cuttings of paper and cooking foil. Rub the pen on the wool and hold near to the pepper. Watch what happens. Now try the other materials. Fill in the chart below.

EXPERIMENT REPORT

Date: *13th December, 1991* Title: *A test to see if stati[illegible]ctrici[illegible]ick things up.*

Diagram

The things I used were *a plastic pen, a woo[illegible]mper and the materials in the table below.*

This is what I did. *I rubbed the [illegible]ool. I held it near each material in turn.*

Material	Picked up	Did not pick up
Pepper	*Yes*	
Salt	*Yes*	
Co[illegible]	*Yes*	
P[illegible]vings	*Yes*	
Paper c[illegible]	*Yes*	
Foil cuttings	*Yes*	

I found out that *static electricity attracted small amounts of each of the materials.*

Questions to answer

1) What is moving electricity called? *Moving electricity is called electric current.*

2) What is "standing still" electricity called? *Standing still electricity [illegible] static electricity.*

3) Can a balloon become charged with static electricity? *Yes a b[illegible] can become charged with static electricity.*

4) How does static electricity affect slow running water? *S[illegible] ele[illegible]city makes slow running tap water bend.*

5) Can static electricity attract paper? *Static electricity ca[illegible]ct paper.*

6) Do you think static electricity could lift he[illegible]ects? *I do not think static electricity could lift heavy objects.*

Problems to solve

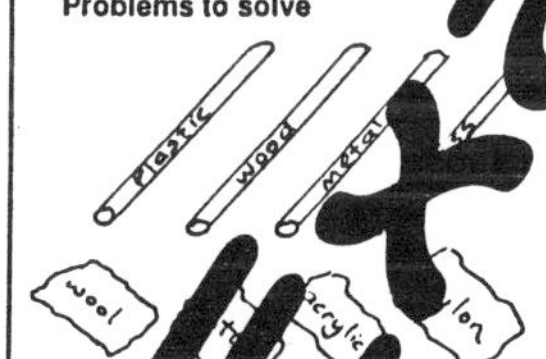

Can you make static electricity using materials other than plastic and wool?

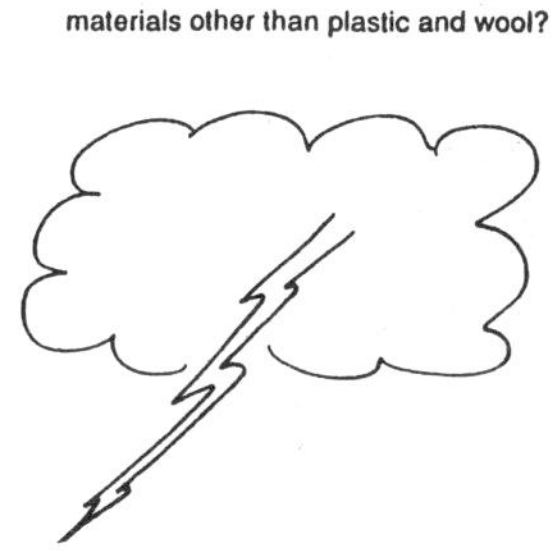

Research the causes and effects of Thunder and Lightening.

Level 3 - HOW CAN YOU MAKE A SIMPLE CIRCUIT? - Teacher's Notes

Equipment needed: (For details of equipment used, refer to equipment page). 4.5 volt battery, two insulated wires with bare ends, two wires with crocodile clips, 2.5 volt torch bulb, 1.5 volt torch bulb, a bulb holder mounted on a wooden block.

Experiment 1: Aim - to help children understand that to make a simple circuit to light a bulb, a circular path has to be created from one side of the battery to the bulb and then from a different part of the bulb back to the battery.

It may help the non-specialist teacher to think of this in terms of simple plumbing or pipe work. The battery represents a pump pushing water (electricity) along a pipe (the wire) through a device (the bulb) and back to the starting point. In practice if the circuit is broken, the "electricity" can not be pushed through the wire. It may need to be pointed out that the circuit will not be complete unless the ends of the wires are tightly held against the battery terminals or the appropriate metal points of the bulb.

Careful examination of the transparent part of the bulb will reveal a very fine high resistance wire. This gives off light when electricity is passed through it. Different wires give different intensity of light.
A hand lens may be useful here, but do not observe closely when bulb is lit.

Experiment 2: Aim - to help the children understand that not all bulbs function in exactly the same way.

In this experiment, the children are required to make a simple circuit using wires with crocodile clips (for easy attachment) and a simple bulb holder (again for ease of electrical contact). Two different torch bulbs should be offered to the children, a 2.5 volt bulb and a 3.5 volt bulb. (They can be identified by the writing on the metal part of the bulbs). They will discover that one bulb will glow more brightly than the other. This is due to different types of high resistance wire being used in the internal construction of the bulbs.

Questions to answer

The questions emphasize the need for electricity to have a circular path to move round before electric current will flow. It is only when electrical current is moving that an electrical device (e.g. a bulb lighting) will function.

Problems to solve

These extension activities are for children who want to develop further the idea of using a simple circuit to make bulbs light up.

Experiment 1 - How can you light a bulb?

You need a 4.5v battery, two wires and a torch bulb. Hold the wires tightly onto the bulb, one at the side and one underneath. Ask a friend to hold the other ends of the wires onto the metal parts of the battery. What happens?

EXPERIMENT REPORT

Date: *16th January* Title: *Lighting a bulb [illegible] battery and wires.*

Diagram

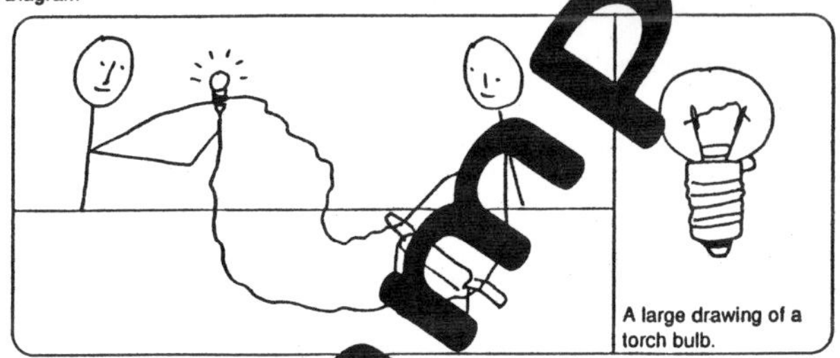

The things I used were *a 4.5v [illegible], [illegible]o wires and a torch bulb.*

This is what I did *I held [illegible] wires [illegible]to the bulb. My friend held the other ends of the wires onto the b[illegible]*

The bulb lit w[illegible]n *all th[illegible]res were held tightly in place.*

The bu[illegible] when [illegible]e of the wires was loose.*

If I look carefu[illegible] the bulb I can see *some glass and a tiny curly wire.*

Draw a picture of this in the space provided.

Experiment 2 - Are all bulbs the same?

You need a 4.5v battery, 2 wires with crocodile clips, a bulb holder and two torch bulbs. Screw one bulb into the holder. Make a simple circuit to light the bulb. Now try the other bulb. What happens?

EXPERIMENT REPORT

Date: *17th January* Title: *A test to see if two b[illegible]ht up in the same way*

Diagram

The things I used were *a 4.5v [illegible], [illegible]res with crocodile clips, two bulbs and a bulb holder.*

This is what I did. *I scre[illegible]ulb into the holder. I made a circuit with the wires and the bul[illegible]hen I tried the other bulb.*

When I li[illegible]s I noticed *one bulb was brighter than the other.*

The croco[illegible]roved the circuit because *they held the wires tightly in place.*

The bulb holder improved the circuit because *the bulb was connected tightly to the wires.*

Questions to answer

1) How can you tell if electricity is flowing through a bulb? *The bulb lights when electricity is flowing through it.*

2) What makes electricity flow or move? *A battery in a circuit mak[illegible] flow.*

3) What do you need to make a simple circuit? *To make a simp[illegible]it you need a battery, two wires and a bulb.*

4) Do wires have to be held on tight or will slack wires do? *[illegible]ires [illegible]t be held on tight to make a circuit work properly.*

5) Are all bulbs the same? *No, all bulbs are not the sam[illegible]e are brighter than others.*

6) What happens to a battery when a bulb is [illegible] for hours? *If a bulb is left on for a long time the battery will run dow[illegible]*

Problems to solve

Can you make two bulbs light at the same time using one battery?

Can you make [illegible] model with lights that work?

Level 3 - HOW DOES A SWITCH WORK? - Teacher's Notes

Equipment needed: (For details of equipment used, refer to equipment page). Six wires with crocodile clips, two paper clip switches, two bulbs in holders, two 4.5 volt batteries.

Experiment 1: Aim - to help children understand how a simple switch works.

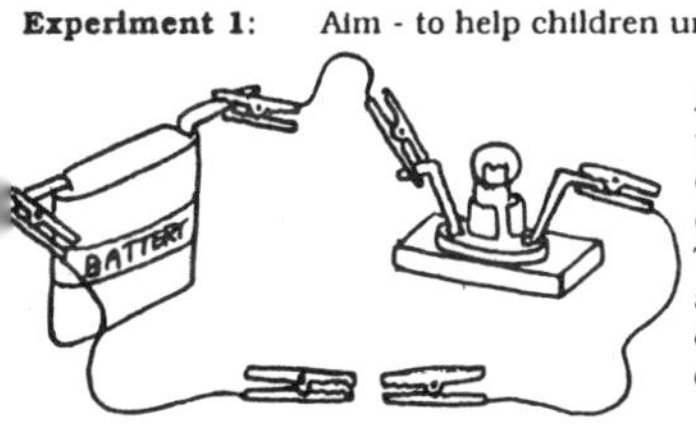

A simple circuit is made to light the bulb using three wires. By disconnecting the clips in the centre of the longest lead, the circuit is broken and the light goes out. This 'gap' is in effect a simple switch. If a simple paper clip switch is fitted into the circuit at this point, the bulb will now be controlled by pushing the paper clip down.

Experiment 2: Aim - to help the children to understand that simple circuits with a switch are of practical use to us.

In this experiment children are asked to send messages across the classroom using morse-code, an example of which is found on the first page of the investigation.

Questions to answer

These questions emphasize that a simple switch is merely a mechanical means of creating a physical gap in an electrical circuit.

Problems to solve

These extension activities are for those children who would like to investigate further the concept of using a switch. Many different kinds of switches are available. Some examples could be found for the children to experiment with. Opportunity is given for the children to come up with their own design.

Experiment 1 - Can you make a simple switch?

Join two wires together using crocodile clips. Now use this 'long' wire in a circuit to light a bulb from a 4.5v battery. Switch the bulb on and off by making a gap. Now try adding a simple paper clip switch into your circuit.

EXPERIMENT REPORT

Date: *23rd February* Title: *How to make a s[illegible] a simple circuit.*

Diagram

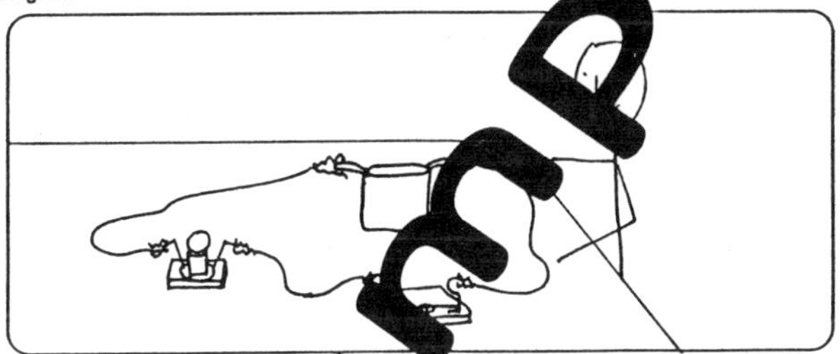

The things I used were *three [illegible] crocodile clips, a battery, a bulb in a holder, and a paper clip swit[illegible]*

This is what I did. *I m[illegible] a cir[illegible] and lit the bulb. Then I separated two wires and made a gap.*

The bulb [illegible] lit [illegible]hen *[illegible] were no gaps in the circuit.*

The bulb [illegible] hen *a gap was made in the circuit.*

I think the bulb came on because *the electricity from the battery flowed through the bulb and back to the battery again.*

Experiment 2 - Can messages be sent using a switch?

Make a circuit to light a bulb using a paper clip switch. Ask a friend to do the same. Use morse-code to send messages across the classroom. Is it possible?

EXPERIMENT REPORT

Date: *24th February* Title: *A test to see if messag[illegible] [illegible]ent using a switch.*

Diagram

The things I used were *a batt[illegible] [illegible]b and holder, a paper clip switch and some wires.*

This is what I did. *I made a c[illegible] with a switch in. I switched the bulb on and off using the switc[illegible]*

Morse code lette[illegible] [illegible]ent by *using 'long' or 'short' flashes of the bulb.*

W[illegible] *quite difficult* to send messages in this way.

The mes[illegible] sent was *Help! We are sinking.*

Questions to answer

1) What would you need to make a simple circuit? *I would need a battery, some wires and a bulb to make a simple circuit.*

2) How can you put a light on or off? *You can put a light on and of[illegible] [illegible] switch.*

3) How does a switch work? *A switch works by making [illegible] in a circuit.*

4) Can electricity from a 4.5v battery jump across a gap? *[illegible] can not jump across a gap.*

5) What is 'Morse Code' used for? *Morse code is use[illegible] [illegible]ding messages.*

6) Who uses 'Morse Code'? *Ships and the [illegible]legram service use morse code.*

Problems to solve

Switches come in different shapes and sizes. Try different types in a simple circuit. Investigate how they work.

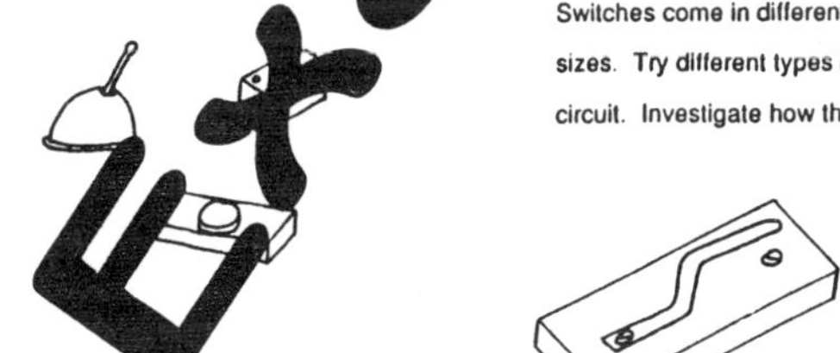

Draw and m[illegible] a switch of your own design.

Level 3 - WHAT IS A WIRE? - Teacher's Notes

Equipment needed: (For details of equipment used, refer to equipment page.) 4.5 volt battery, three wires with crocodile clips, a bulb and holder, a plastic covered wire with bare ends, a number of small objects, such as a ruler, a rubber, a paper clip, a drawing pin etc.

Experiment 1: Aim - to help children understand that electricity passes through some materials more easily than it does others.

A simple circuit is constructed with a gap between two crocodile clips. Various objects are connected to the clips to complete the circuit. A table is completed showing which materials conducted the electricity and which did not. It will be noted that it is mainly metal objects which conduct electricity.

Experiment 2: Aim - to help the children understand that wires are often constructed from an electrical conductor protected by an electrical insulator.

The children are asked to investigate which parts of a plastic insulated wire are able to conduct electricity. It will be found the circuit will only be complete when crocodile clips are attached to the metal parts of the wire. Try asking children to pass electricity through unstripped wire. What ideas are forth-coming?

Questions to answer

These questions emphasize the terms 'conductor' and 'insulator'.

Problems to solve

These activities are for those children who would like to investigate further the conduction of electricity. Passing electricity through a pencil will demonstrate a poor conductor. When working with different metals ensure all have clean surfaces for good electrical contact.

Experiment 1 - Which materials conduct electricity?

Find a 4.5v battery, a bulb and holder, three wires with crocodile clips and a number of small objects such as a ruler, a rubber, a paper clip, a drawing pin etc. Make a circuit which makes electricity pass through one object. Does the bulb light? Try the other objects. Fill in the table.

EXPERIMENT REPORT

Date: *16th March* Title: *A test to see whic[illegible] materi[illegible] [illegible]uct electricity.*

Diagram

The things I used were wires, [illegible]ttery, a bulb and holder and some objects.

This is what I did. *I made [illegible] [illegible]e c[illegible]uit with a gap. I placed the objects in the gap. I looked to see if the b[illegible] [illegible] up.*

Object	P[illegible]sed electricity through = Conductor	Did not pass electricity = Insulator
r[illegible]r		✓
[illegible]cil		✓
[illegible]ule[illegible]		✓
[illegible] clip	✓	
[illegible]g pin	✓	
p[illegible]		✓
book		✓
scissors	✓	

I think all of the conductors were made of *metal.*

Experiment 2 - Which parts of a wire conduct electricity?

Find a 4.5v battery, a bulb and holder, three wires with crocodile clips and a plastic wire with bare metal ends. Make a simple circuit and test the bulb. Now include the plastic wire with bare metal ends in the circuit. What happens?

EXPERIMENT REPORT

Date: *17th March* Title: *A test to see if wi[illegible] is a c[illegible] of electricity.*

Diagram

The things I used were *wires, a batter[illegible], [illegible]ulb and holder and plastic coated wire with bare ends.*

This is what I did. *I made [illegible]i[illegible]uit [illegible]h a gap. I fastened the wire in the gap and looked at the bulb.*

With the crocodile clips [illegible] to the bare metal ends of the wire the bulb *lit up.*

With th[illegible] [illegible]ocodile cli[illegible] [illegible]stened to the plastic cover on the wire the bulb *did not light up.*

Wi[illegible] [illegible]e [illegible] on a m[illegible]l end and the other clip on the plastic cover the bulb *d[illegible] [illegible]ght.*

The wire [illegible] [illegible]ducts when *electricity is passed through the metal part on the inside.*

Questions to answer

1) Will electricity pass through all materials? *Electricity will not pass through all materials.*

2) What is a conductor? *A conductor is material which electricit[illegible] [illegible] [illegible]ss through.*

3) What is an insulator? *An insulator is material electric[illegible] [illegible] not pass through.*

4) How did you know if electricity was flowing in your circu[illegible] [illegible] *electricity was flowing when the bulb lit up.*

5) What is a wire? *A wire is a long thin strand o[illegible] [illegible]*

6) Why does a mains wire usually have a pla[illegible] cover? *Mains wires are covered in plastic to protect people from electri[illegible]*

Problems to solve

Will electricity pass through the lead in the centre of a pencil?

Are all meta[illegible] [illegible]od conductors of electricity?

Level 4 - HOW CAN ELECTRICITY HELP US? (Part 1) - Teacher's Notes

Equipment needed: 4.5v battery, paper clip switch, 4 wires with clips, an 8cm nail, 1m length of plastic coated wire, a buzzer, a bell, a bent wire coat hanger, a copper washer and a wooden base (see equipment notes).

Experiment 1: Aim - to help the children understand that a magnetic force can be created by passing a current through a coil of insulated wire.

Children may find difficulty in making a tight coil of wire around the nail, so it may be useful to prepare this for them. The coil can be held in place by sellotape. It is important to ensure the nail is not already magnetic, before the current is applied.
This experiment is a demonstration of the magnetic effects caused when electricity is passed through a coil of wire.

Experiment 2: Aim - to help the children realise how the magnetic effects of electricity can be made to work for us.

It is important to realise that the buzzer will only work if connected to the battery the correct way round. The red wire on the buzzer must be connected to the positive (+) terminal on the battery. To connect these the wrong way round will not harm the buzzer but it will fail to function.

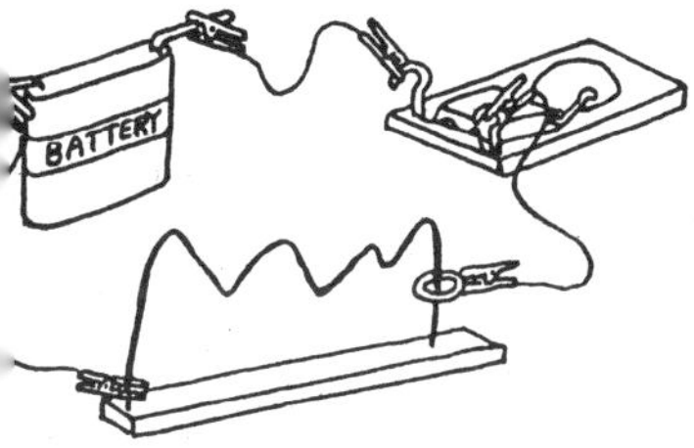

A simple game of skill can be made as shown in this diagram.

Questions to answer

The questions draw out the fact that electricity can be used to create a controllable magnetic field and by doing so, can be used to power machines that are useful to us.

Problems to solve

This extension activities are for those children who wish to explore further the magnetic effects of electricity.

Experiment 1 - Can you make an electric magnet?

You need a 4.5v battery, a paper clip switch, three wires with crocodile clips, an 8cm nail and 1m of fine plastic coated wire. Check the nail does not act like a magnet. Wrap the wire tightly round the nail. Make the circuit shown on page 1. Hold the nail close to a paper clip and press the switch. What happens?

EXPERIMENT REPORT

Date: *3/4/91* Title: *How to make ... elect... ...et*

Diagram

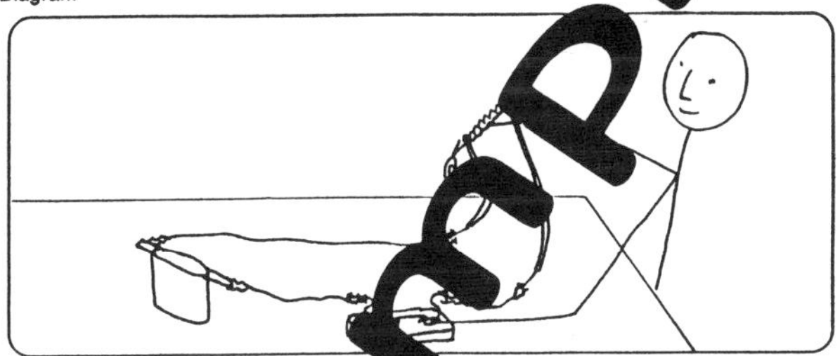

Equipment needed: *I needed ... switch, a nail and some plastic coated wire.*

Method used: *I wrapped the ... und the nail tightly and held it in place with sellotape. I co...cted ... wire to the battery through a switch. When I switched on, the nai... ...p paper clips.*

Observations mad... *...n the battery was switched off the nail sometimes held onto the ...per clips ... would only pick up paper clips with the battery conne...d.*

How ... ...per cli... ...ill your electric magnet lift? *My electric magnet picked up 12 pape... in ... go.*

Experiment 2 - Can you make a buzzer or bell ring?

You need a 4.5v battery, a push button switch, four wires with clips, a buzzer, a bell, a copper washer and a bent coat hanger on a wooden base. Make a circuit with a battery, bell and switch. Make a circuit with battery, buzzer and switch. Include the wire coat hanger in one circuit. Can you make a game of skill?

EXPERIMENT REPORT

Date: *4/4/91* Title: *An experiment ... ...uzze... ...d bells.*

Diagram

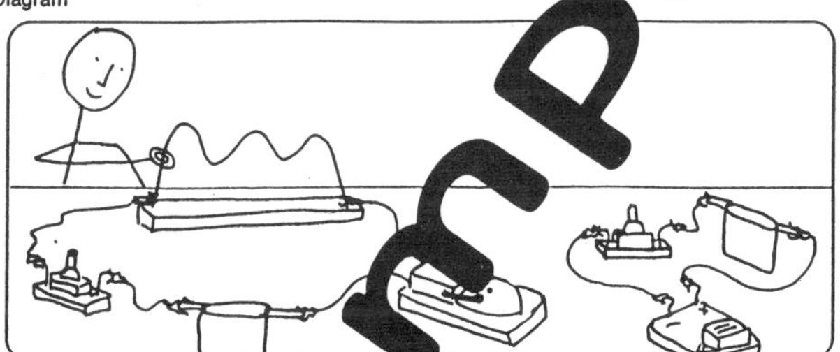

Equipment needed: *I neede... ...ire... ...ires, a buzzer, a bell and a bent coat hanger.*

Methods used: *I made ... ...ir... with the bell. Pressing the switch made the bell ring. The switc... ...the buzzer buzz.*

Observ...ns ...de: *Th... ...uzzer had to be connected up a certain way to make the ...z... work. ...e bell could be connected up any way.*

How did ... ... a game of skill? *We made a game of skill by moving a metal washer alon... the coat hanger without ringing the bell.*

Questions to answer

1) Why do magnets pick up metal objects? *Magnets pick up metal objects because their magnetic field attracts some metals.*

2) When does a wire have a magnetic field? *A wire has a magnetic f... ...hen electricity is passed through it.*

3) How can you make an electric magnet? *You can make ... electr... ...et by wrapping wire round a nail and passing a current thr...*

4) When does an electric magnet attract metal objects? *An ...ric m...net attracts metal objects when a current is passed through t... ...ire.*

5) What are buzzers and bells used for in the home? *... ...er... ...d bells are used for alarms and doors etc.*

6) What makes an electric buzzer or bell ope...te? *A... ...ctric magnet makes a buzzer or bell operate.*

Problems to solve

How powerful can you ...ke a home made electric m...

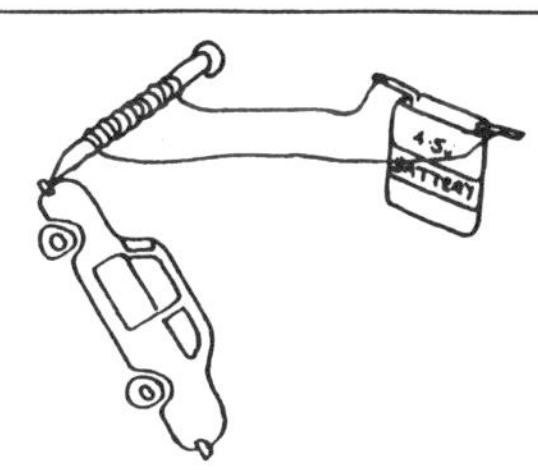

Design and build a burglar alarm which sets off a bell or buzzer.

Level 4 - HOW CAN ELECTRICITY HELP US? (Part 2) - Teacher's Notes

Equipment needed: a 4.5v battery, two wires with clips, a small plate or dish, some wire wool, a small electric motor, some blue-tack and a circle of card (approx. 10cm in diameter).

Experiment 1: Aim - to help children understand that sometimes wire becomes very hot when electricity is passed through it.

SAFETY NOTE : It is advisable that the teacher carries out this activity before the children try, in order to observe the effect and ascertain for his / herself the safety measures needed to be taken with their particular group of children.

The experiment works best when one individual strand of wire wool can be isolated and the clips are held against it at approx. 1 - 2 cm apart, e.g.

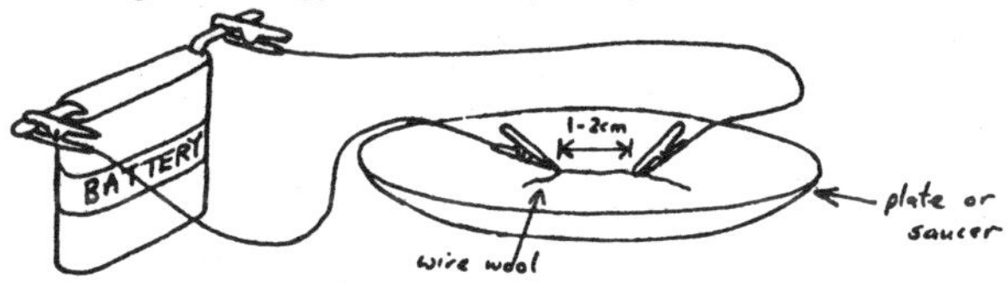

Experiment 2: Aim - to help children realise that electricity is needed to make an electric motor run.

The point can be drawn out that when the motor is connected to the battery, the motor rotates in a certain direction and when the wires are reversed the motor rotates in the opposite direction.

Questions to answer

The questions draw out the fact that the heating effects of electricity and the motor effects of electricity can be used in machines that perform useful work for us.

Problems to solve

Secondary sources can be used to research various applications of fuses in circuits.

The second activity is a design technology task which demands that the children design build and test a simple lifting device.

Experiment 1 - Can you make a wire hot?

You need a 4.5v battery, two wires with clips, a plate and some wire wool. Remove 1 strand only from the wire wool and place on the plate. Connect the wires to the battery and use them to touch the wire wool. Try long lengths and short lengths of wire wool. What happens?

EXPERIMENT REPORT

Date: *19/6/91* Title: *An experiment to inv[illegible] how to make a wire hot.*

Diagram

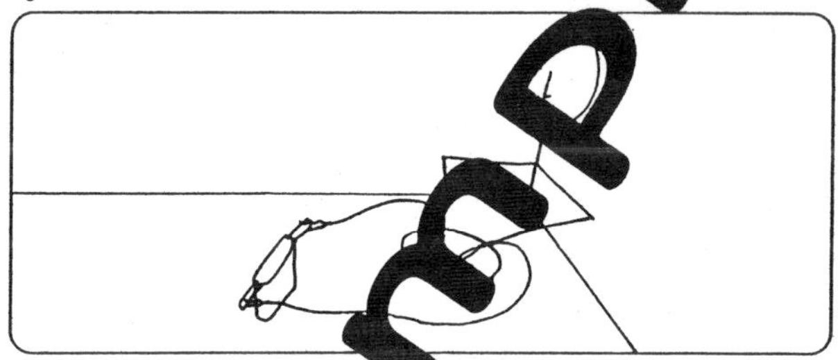

Equipment needed: *I needed [illegible] two wires and some wire wool.*

Method used: *I took one stra[illegible] of [illegible]ire wool and held it between two clips. Then I connected th[illegible] clips t[illegible] battery.*

Observations mad[illegible] *[illegible]ire wool glowed very brightly and then seemed to burn away.*

Wha[illegible] greate[illegible] length of wire wool to heat up? *The greatest length of wire wo[illegible] he[illegible] up was 10cm long.*

Experiment 2 - Can you make an electric motor run?

You need a 4.5v battery, two wires, a small electric motor, some blue tack and a circle of card. Draw a pattern on the card and fasten it using blue tack to the axle on the motor. Connect the motor to the battery. What happens?

EXPERIMENT REPORT

Date: *20/6/91* Title: *An experimen[illegible] [illegible]vesti[illegible] how to get an electric motor to run.*

Diagram

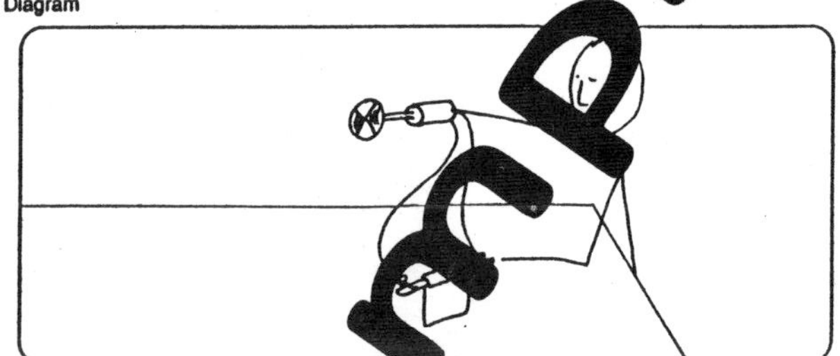

Equipment needed: *I neede[illegible] [illegible] two wires, an electric motor, some blue tack and a circle of card.*

Method used: *I colour[illegible] the c[illegible] and fastened it onto the axle of the motor. When the circuit was made [illegible] battery the motor spun the card very quickly.*

Observati[illegible] made: *[illegible] the card spun round the colours on the pattern blurred toget[illegible].*

What [illegible] you reverse the wires on the battery? *When you reverse the wires on the batt[illegible] the motor spins in the opposite direction.*

Questions to answer

1) What is an electric heater? *An electric heater is a fire powered by electricity.*

2) How are electric heaters used in the home? *Electric heaters are sometimes used to heat a room or heat water in an electric kettle.*

3) What is an electric motor? *An electric motor is an engine po[illegible] b[illegible] electricity.*

4) Which machines in the home use electric motors? *Machines [illegible] hairdryers, washing machines and vacuum cleaners use electric [illegible]*

5) How do you make a very thin wire hot? *A thin [illegible] can b[illegible] made hot by passing electricity through it.*

6) How do you make an electric motor change [illegible]? *An e[illegible]tric motor can change direction if the wires to the bat[illegible] are r[illegible]rsed.*

Problems to solve

Research what fuses are, how they work and what the[illegible] used for.

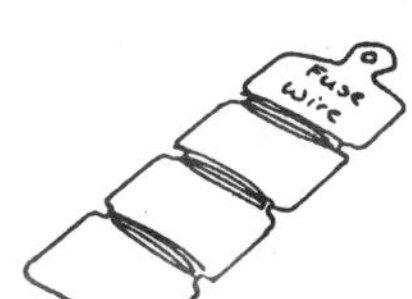

Design and make a simple lifting device using an electric motor. How much will it lift?

Level 4 - HOW CAN SWITCHES CONTROL ELECTRICAL DEVICES? - Teacher's Notes

Equipment needed: a 4.5v battery, 4 paper clip switches, 2 bulbs in holders, an electric motor, 8 wires with clips, green and red coloured tissue paper.

Experiment 1: Aim - to help children understand how two switches can be used to control two bulbs from one power source.

The equipment must be wired up exactly as shown in the drawing on page 2 of this investigation. Toy cars can be used to help the children re-create a road works scene and discover what problems occur when the traffic lights are put into use.

Experiment 2: Aim - to help the children understand how switches can be used to reverse the action of an electric motor.

The equipment must be wired up exactly as shown in the drawing on page 3 of this investigation. It may be helpful to the children if each switch is given a number from 1 to 4. It will be found that only two of the six permetations will activate the motor and of these two, it will be found the motor operates in opposite directions.

Questions to answer

The points drawn out in the questions illustrate the sort of work switches do for us.

Problems to solve

These two design technology activities are for those children who wish to extend their knowledge of the work switches can do for us in the operation of simple working machines.

Experiment 1 - Can you make a simple traffic light?

You need a 4.5v battery, two paper-clip switches, two bulbs in holders, 6 wires with clips and red and green tissue paper. Cover the bulbs with tissue. Connect up the wires as shown in the picture below. Can you operate a traffic light?

EXPERIMENT REPORT

Date: *23/9/90* Title: *An experiment to test a ... traffic light circuit.*

Diagram

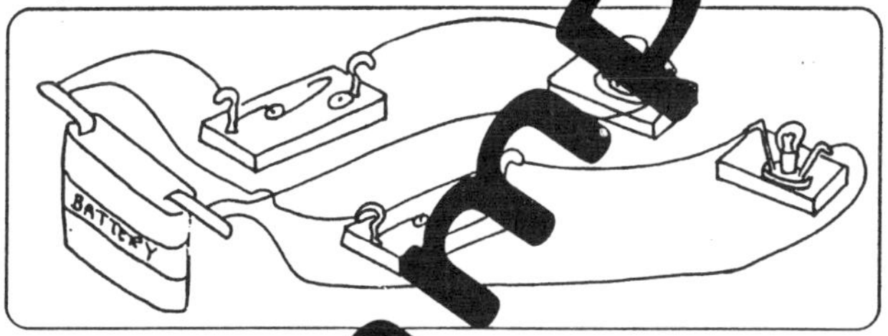

Equipment needed: *I needed a ... switches, 6 wires and 2 bulbs in holders.*

Method used: *The bulbs ... re connected as shown in the diagram above. Tissue paper was used to mak... ...ghts.*

Observatio... *One ...tch controlled the red light. The other switch control... ...greenli...t.*

Use toy cars to ... a road works scene. What problems do you have? *For the road works scene to work properly we would need two sets of traffic lights.*

Experiment 2 - Can you make an electric motor change direction?

You need a 4.5v battery, four paper-clip switches, an electric motor, and 8 wires with clips. Connect the wires as shown in the picture below. Which switches make the motor work?

EXPERIMENT REPORT

Date: *24/9/91* Title: *An experiment to ... control of an electric motor*

Diagram

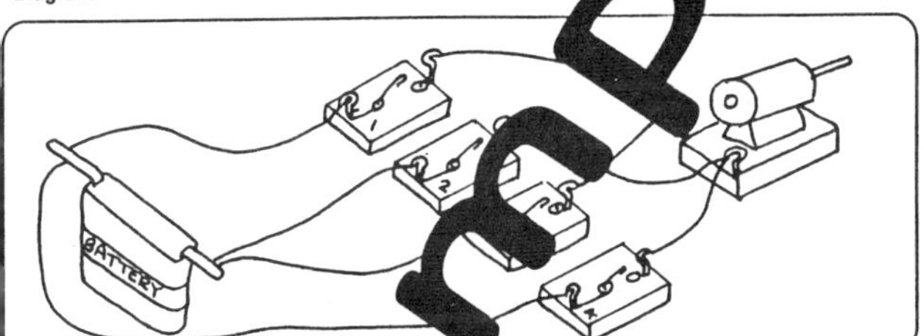

Equipment needed: *I needed a ... switches, 8 wires with clips and an electric motor.*

Method used: *I wired the swi... the motor as shown in the diagram above. I pressed the switch... see when the motor worked.*

Switch (1) an... pressed = *... worked*

Switch (1) ... (3) ...ssed = *nothing happened*

Switch ... pressed = *...thing happened*

Switch (2) and (3) pressed = *nothing happened*

Switch (2) and (4) pressed = *nothing happened*

Switch (3) and (4) pressed = *motor worked*

Which switch... the motor turn clockwise? *Switch (1) and (2) made the motor turn clockwise.*

Which switches made the motor turn anti-clockwise? *Switch (3) and (4) made the motor turn anti-clockwise.*

Questions to answer

1) What may you use a switch for in the home? *A switch is used to control lights in the home.*

2) How does a switch work? *A switch works by opening and closi... ...p i... circuit.*

3) Why might you need to use more than one switch? *More than ... ...itch is sometimes needed to make the circuits you require to operate your ...ctrical devices.*

4) How many switches did you need to operate your traf...? *T... switches were needed to operate the traffice light.*

5) How many switches did you need to reverse th... elec... ...tor? *Four switches were needed to reverse the electric motor.*

6) What jobs do some switches in a real c... do? *S...hes in a car work the wind-screen wipers, the lights, the horn, ...icators etc.*

Problems to solve

Can you design a traffic lig... ... will run the co...ct seque... ... Red, Ambe... ...d ...en?

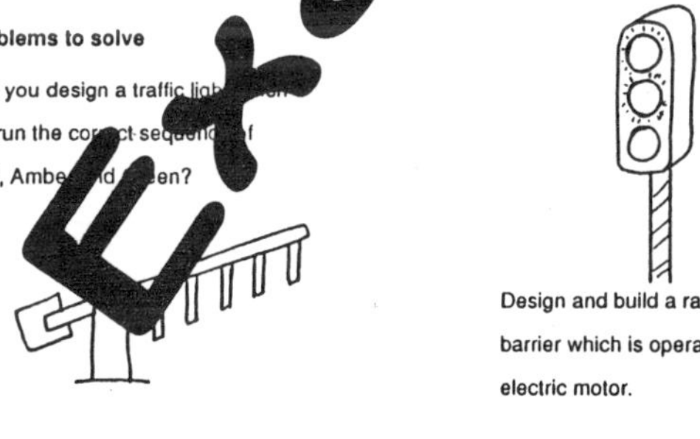

Design and build a railway crossing barrier which is operated by an electric motor.

Level 5 - WHAT ARE LOGIC GATES? - Teacher's Notes

Equipment needed: 4.5v battery, a bulb in holder, 3 push button switches, a paper clip switch, a buzzer, six wires with clips.

Experiment 1: Aim - to help children understand how a very simple "And Gate" circuit works.

Logic Gates were formerly electronic systems which used switches operated by electric magnets which opened and closed electrical paths in different directions. A gate is therefore a point at which, a logical decision has been made to choose the path the electricity takes.

This technology is now used in micro-processor systems and is the fundamental concept in the design of computers.

This experiment illustrates a simple "and" gate circuit. It is important to connect the circuit up exactly as shown in the diagram on page 2 of this investigation for the experiment to work.

The point to be drawn out is one switch and another need to be operated for the circuit to function.

Experiment 2: Aim - to help the children understand how a very simple "Not Gate" circuit works.

This experiment illustrates a simple "Not Gate" circuit. It is important to connect the circuit up exactly as shown in the diagram on page 3 of this investigation for the experiment to work.

The point to be drawn out is that one switch but not the other need to be operated for the circuit to function.

Questions to answer

The questions require the children to think carefully about the operation of each of the circuits that they have experimented with.

Problems to solve

These activities offer those children who are able to apply their knowledge of AND, OR, and NOT gate circuits to a simple logic quiz game or home made burglar alarm.

Experiment 1 - Can you construct an AND GATE circuit?

You need a 4.5v battery, a push button switch, a paper clip switch, a buzzer and four wires with clips. Make up the circuit shown below. When does the burglar alarm buzzer sound? (N.B. the buzzer must be connected in the correct way).

EXPERIMENT REPORT

Date: *14/10/91* Title: *An experiment to investig... AND GATE circuit.*

Diagram

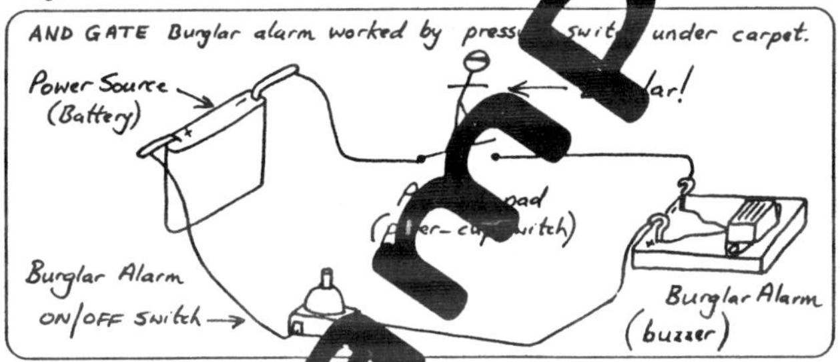

Equipment needed: *I needed ...ba...ery ...our wires with clips, a push switch, a paper clip switch and a buzz...*

Method used: *I mad... ...cuit shown in the diagram. When both switches were on th... ...uzzer bu...ed.*

Obser... ...de: *T... on/off switch controlled the burglar alarm. With the alarm ... ...d t... burglar would sound the alarm when he stood on the mat.*

The burglar alarm will only light up when *the pressure switch AND the on/off switch are operated.*

Experiment 2 - Can you construct a NOT GATE circuit?

You need a 4.5v battery, a bulb in holder, a push button switch, a paper clip switch and a buzzer and six wires with clips. Make up the circuit shown below. Hold the paper clip switch down (this would be the window closed) and switch on the circuit. What happens? How can th... ...m be set off? (N.B. The buzzer must be connected in the correct way).

EXPERIMENT REPORT

Date: *15/10/91* Title: *An experiment to investig... NOT GATE circuit.*

Diagram

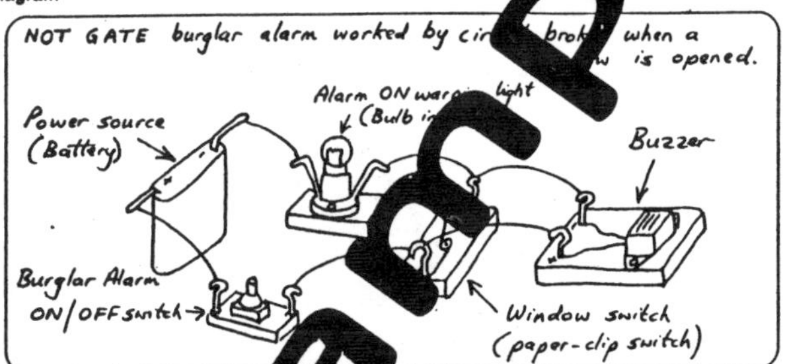

Equipment needed: *I needed a ba... ...n push switch, a paper clip switch, a buzzer, a bulb in holde... ...d six wires with clips.*

Method used: *I made the ... ...own in the diagram.*

How do you ...ow ...hen th... ...uit is switched on? *I know when the circuit is switche... ...n ...cause t... warning light glows.*

When th... ...lip ...ch was held down (in real life the window switch closed) and the circuit was switch... ...on *the warning light glowed brightly.*

When the paper clip switch was opened (in real life the window opened) and the circuit was switched on *the warning light dimmed and the buzzer sounded.*

Questions to answer

1) What is a gate in a circuit? *A gate in a circuit can be another name for a switch.*

2) When does electricity flow in an AND GATE circuit? *Electricity flo... i... AND GATE circuit when one switch and another are closed.*

3) When does electricity flow in an OR GATE circuit? *Electricit... ...in an OR GATE circuit when one switch or another is closed.*

4) When does electricity flow in a NOT GATE circuit? *Ele...city ...vs in an NOT GATE circuit when one switch and not the other ...losed.*

5) What can these circuits be used for? *These circ...its can ... to control burglar alarms and computers.*

6) What is logic? *Logic is when the brai... ...sed to reason or work things out.*

Problems to solve

Can you make a logic game which lights a bulb through three push button swi...

Can you make a burglar alarm circuit which has a pressure pad OR a window switch to set off the alarm?

Level 5 - CAN YOU CONSTRUCT A CIRCUIT FROM A PLAN? - Teacher's Notes

Equipment needed: a 4.5v battery, 2 bulbs in holders, 4 wires with clips.

Experiment 1: Aim - to help children understand what is meant by a "series" circuit and construct one from a circuit diagram.

It is important that this circuit is connected up exactly as shown in the diagram.

It will most likely be found that the bulbs will not glow very brightly. A similar single bulb in the same circuit will glow more brightly.

Experiment 2: Aim - to help the children understand what is meant by a "parallel" circuit and construct one from a circuit diagram.

t is important that this circuit is connected up xactly as shown in he diagram.

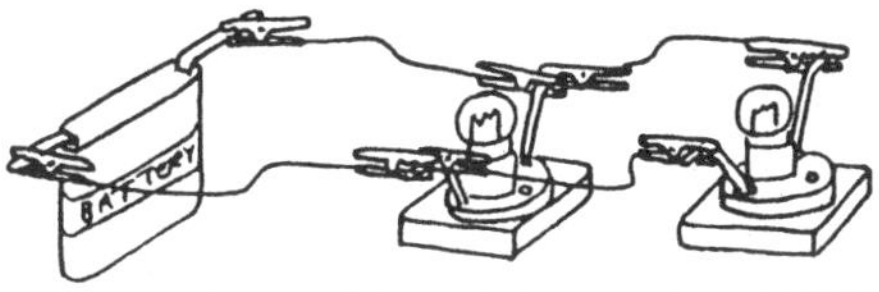

t will be found that two bulbs connected in a parallel circuit glow more brightly than the ame two bulbs connected in the series circuit. This is because a greater "electrical ressure", is applied to the individual bulbs in the parallel circuit. In the "series" circuit he "electrical pressure" is less, because the same current flows through the resistance ffered by both bulbs.

n the "parallel" circuit, the two bulbs will glow more brightly but will run the battery down n a relatively short time.

n the "series" circuit, the bulbs will glow dimly but the battery will last for a relatively onger time.

uestions to answer

he "questions to answer" draw the pupil's attention to the use of wiring diagrams, specially in "series" and "parallel" circuits.

roblems to solve

hese extension activities are for those pupils who wish to extend their knowledge and nderstanding of "series" and "parallel" circuits.

Experiment 1 - Can you construct a "Series" circuit from a plan?

You need a 4.5v battery, two bulbs in holders and three wires with crocodile clips. Construct this circuit.

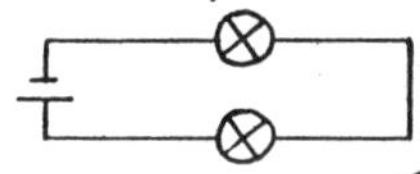

EXPERIMENT REPORT

Date: *25/11/91* Title: *An experiment to [illegible]tigate [illegible]lbs lit up in a 'series' circuit.*

Diagram

Equipment needed: *I needed a [illegible] three wires with clips and two bulbs in holders.*

Method used: *I conne[illegible] the [illegible]bs to the battery as shown in the circuit diagram.*

Observat[illegible] made: *Th[illegible]wo bulbs lit up when the circuit was complete. They did n[illegible] sh[illegible] very [illegible]ightly.*

Make a [illegible]nly one bulb connected. Which circuit had the brightest lights? Why?

The circuit [illegible]h one bulb shone most brightly. I think one battery has not enough electricity to make two bulbs shine brightly.

Experiment 2 - Can you construct a "Parellel" circuit from a plan?

You need a 4.5v battery, two bulbs in holders and four wires with clips. Construct this circuit.

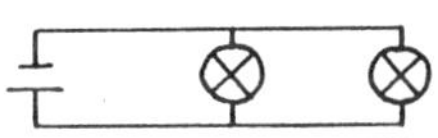

EXPERIMENT REPORT

Date: *26/11/91* Title: *An experi[illegible]t to [illegible]ate bulbs lit up in a 'parallel' circuit.*

Diagram

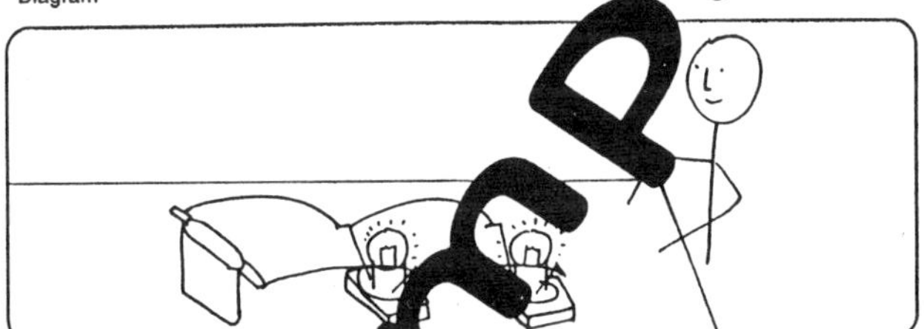

Equipment needed: *I needed a [illegible]ttery, t[illegible] bulbs in holders and four wires with clips.*

Method used: *I made the ci[illegible]own in the wiring diagram.*

Observa[illegible]s made: *[illegible] two bulbs in this circuit seemed to shine much brighter than [illegible]bs in t[illegible]series circuit.*

M[illegible]cuit wi[illegible]nly one bulb connected. Which circuit had the brightest lights? Why?

The circ[illegible]h one bulb was just brighter than the one with two. I think more electricity flows in a parallel circuit than a series circuit.

Questions to answer

1) What is an electrician? *An electrician is a person who works with electricity and wires.*

2) How do electricians know where to put wires? *Electricians know [illegible] wires because they follow a plan.*

3) Why are drawings not used on wiring diagrams? *Drawi[illegible]uld [illegible] up too much space on a wiring diagram.*

4) How are bulbs wired in "series"? *Bulbs are wired i[illegible]hen the wires go from one bulb to another making a circular path.*

5) How are bulbs wired in "parallel"? *Bulbs are wire[illegible]s' when one bulb is wired directly onto another bulb.*

6) Which circuit do you think would run the b[illegible]ry down most quickly? *I think a parallel circuit would run the batter[illegible]ost quickly.*

Problems to solve

Can you construct "series" and "parallel" circuits with three bulbs?

Can y[illegible] w[illegible]g diagrams of "series" an[illegible]arallel" circuits with four bulbs?

Level 5 - CAN YOU VARY THE FLOW OF ELECTRICITY IN A CIRCUIT? - Teacher's Note

Equipment needed: a 1.5v, a 3v and a 4.5v battery, a bulb and holder, 3 wires with clips, and a pencil split to expose the graphite centre as shown in the diagram.

Experiment 1: Aim - to help the children understand that batteries of different voltage create different flows of electricity in a simple circuit.

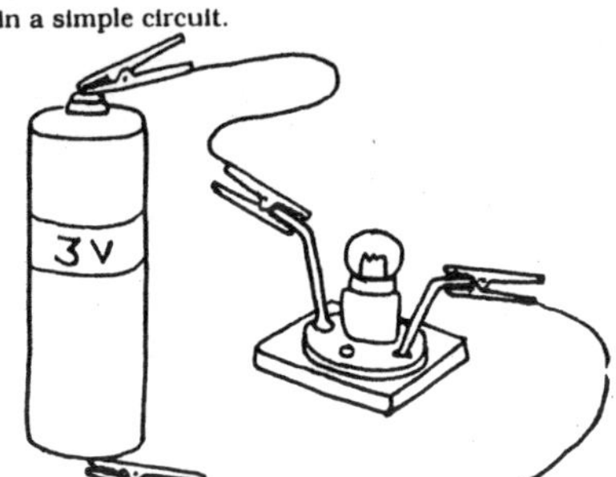

The practical problem of attaching the wires to the correct parts of the batteries may be experienced by the pupils.

The wires should be connected as shown in the diagram. Where crocodile clips can not be attached the wires should merely be held in place.

This experiment will only be a fair test if the batteries used are of a similar age and condition.

Experiment 2: Aim - to help the children understand how the flow of electricity in a circuit can be varied with the use of a partial conductor.

Most materials fall into the categories of a "good" conductor, or a "poor" conductor of electricity. Some materials e.g. carbon, only partially conduct electricity.

The equipment needs to be connected as shown in the diagram. The flow of the electricity can be varied by altering the position of the crocodile clips on the split pencil. When the clips are moved together the bulb glows brighter. When the clips move further apart the bulb dims.

The brightness of the bulb is an indication of how much electricity is flowing in the circuit at that point in time.

Questions to answer

The questions to answer draw together the concepts explored in the experiments carried out.

Problems to solve

These extension activities are for those pupils who wish to explore further varying the flow of electricity in a circuit.

Experiment 1 - How do different sized batteries affect a simple circuit?

You need a 1.5v, a 3v and a 4.5v battery, two wires, a bulb and holder. Construct these circuits in turn. Compare the results.

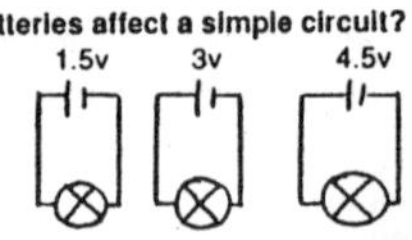

EXPERIMENT REPORT

Date: *9/12/91* Title: *An experiment to investigate [illegible] sizes of battery.*

Diagram

Equipment needed: *I needed [illegible] batteries, two wires, a bulb and a bulb holder.*

Method used: *I made [illegible] circuit with the 1.5v battery. Then I tried the 3v battery. Final[illegible] the 4.5v battery.*

Observations made: *The bulb was brightest with the 4.5v battery. The bulb was di[illegible] with the 1.5v battery.*

Would your test be fair if one battery was near the end of its useful life? *No. All of the batteries need to be in good condition.*

Experiment 2 - How does a partial conductor affect a simple circuit?

You need a 4.5v battery, a bulb and holder, three wires with clips and a pencil split to expose the centre. Construct this circuit. Move the clips along the pencil. What happens?

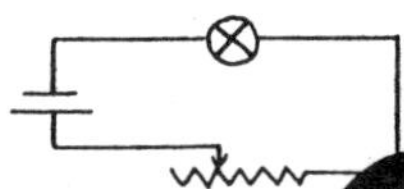

EXPERIMENT REPORT

Date: *10/12/91* Title: *An experiment to [illegible] 'partial conductor' of electricity.*

Diagram

Equipment needed: *I needed [illegible], a bulb in holder, three wires with clips and a split pencil.*

Method used: *I made [illegible] circuit to light the bulb by passing the elctricity through the pe[illegible]tre. I moved the clips up and down the pencil.*

Observations made: *[illegible] pencil did not appear to conduct the electricity very well.*

When [illegible] the brightest? *The bulb was the brightest when the clips on the pencil were close together or touching.*

When was the bulb the dullest? *The bulb was most dull when the clips were at opposite ends of the pencil.*

Questions to answer

1) How do batteries differ? *Batteries differ in size and in how powerful they are.*

2) What does a battery do? *A battery pushes electricity round a cir[illegible]*

3) What do 'volts' tell us? *'Volts' tell us how powerful a batte[illegible].*

4) What is a partial conductor? *A partial conductor is a mater[illegible]hich conducts a little electricity.*

5) How can a split pencil be used to vary the flow of [illegible]tricity in [illegible] simple circuit? *A split pencil can be used to vary the flow of elec[illegible] in a circuit by connecting to the centre material at vari[illegible]tances.*

6) How do you know the flow of electricity i[illegible]aried? *You know the flow of electricity varies because the light [illegible]tly or dimly.*

Problems to solve

What happens if more [illegible]n one battery is used in a ci[illegible]

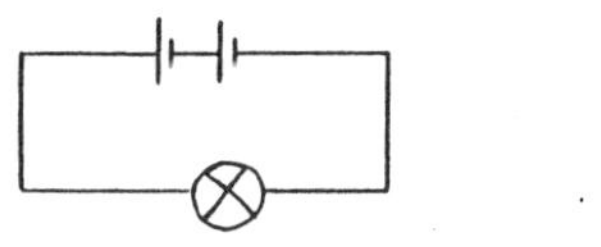

Do some pencils conduct electricity better than others?